DECODING THE DONALD

Trump's Apprenticeship in Politics

SURYA YALAMANCHILI

ISBN-13: 978-0-69265-858-1
Drumpf Publishing

Printed in the United States of America

Designed by Tiffany Wong & Surya Yalamanchili

First Edition

My mother, to whom I owe everything

CONTENTS

INTRODUCTION

Ten years ago, I spent a few months with Donald Trump. That's probably why so many people want to talk to me about this nutty election. While I *do* have a pretty strong opinion on candidate Trump, I felt my first-hand experience with the man wasn't good reason to blabber about him. But I stepped back and realized that maybe I'm more qualified to comment than I first thought.

TRUMP	SURYA
MASTER MARKETER (EXPERT AT SELF PROMOTION + BRANDING)	FORMER PROCTER + GAMBLE BRAND MANAGER (THEY BASICALLY INVENTED MODERN MARKETING + BRANDING)
PERSONALITY UNLIKE OTHER HUMANS	SPENT FEW MONTHS WITH ← THIS PARTICULAR HUMAN
CRUSHING THE REPUBLICAN PARTY PRIMARY	SPENT 1 YEAR + AS A CANDIDATE (2010 DEM. NOMINEE FOR CONGRESS OH-2)
CLAIMS BUSINESS-SUCCESS WILL HELP HIM SOLVE AMERICA'S PROBLEMS	ALSO A BUSINESS TYPE (FORMERLY LINKEDIN, GROUPON, P+G AND A TECH START UP CEO)
STARRING IN THE #1 RATED REALITY TV SHOW : ELECTION 2016	SURVIVED UPS + DOWNS OF STARRING ON THE APPRENTICE

Key Trump things & their bizarre overlap with key Surya things

While I'm not an expert at any one of the things listed above, being able to understand Trump through *all* those lenses and experiences does give me a unique perspective on "The Donald" phenomenon. After I was asked what I thought about Trump's remarkable political rise for the one-thousandth time, I decided to write this book.

∞β∞

It's the folks exasperated by his candidacy that most often ask me about Trump and they're typically pretty shocked that he's leading the race. I'm not surprised by Trump's staggering success. The last CNN poll of 2015 had Trump atop the Republican primary with twice the support of his closest competitor, Ted Cruz. On the way to the top, Trump has mocked John McCain for being a prisoner of war, proposed a blanket ban on all Muslims entering the US, and implied that most Mexican immigrants were criminals. Despite—or fueled by—these statements, Trump surged ahead of the field and hasn't looked back.

At first Trump's campaign seemed like just a way to get free attention and was viewed skeptically. Once he got that attention, his resulting success was quickly explained away as a temporary reaction to outsized press coverage. That evolved into the conventional wisdom that his success in the polls would fade once the novelty wore off, much like it had for Herman Cain and Michele Bachmann before him. Nope.

Trump's nose for attention is second to none. Whether by virtue of slapping his name on anything that could be sold, headlining a reality TV show, or calling Rosie O'Donnell a fat pig—finding ways to get people to talk about Trump has always been what Trump does best. Even with the high bar of past media spectacles to clear, this presidential campaign is undoubtedly his best work.

While many still dismiss Trump's run as a gimmick, his staying power has certainly quieted that talk. Many also seem to believe that Trump is disingenuous and intentionally stoking controversy by saying things he doesn't believe. Yet, I think Trump means what he says and, further, he and his rhetoric are a pitch perfect complement to the current times. While some see Trump's candidacy as proof this is actually "end of times," I'm more sanguine.

The book that follows puts *the Donald Trump I know*, in the context of *the America I know*. I won't be focusing as much on whether Donald Trump is racist, sexist, or some of the more tabloid-esque headlines. That being said…

Trump has never actually said that his main opponent, Ted Cruz, is ineligible to be president. What he said was, "I'd hate to see something like that get in his way, but a lot of people are talking about it." In Trump style, then, let me tell a few stories that are most certainly not me claiming that Trump is racist or sexist. All I'm saying is that I'd hate to see something like that get in his way—because a lot of people are talking about it.

Donald J. Trump
@realDonaldTrump

I refuse to call Megyn Kelly a bimbo, because that would not be politically correct. Instead I will only call her a lightweight reporter!

RETWEETS 3,844   LIKES 10,076

6:44 AM - 27 Jan 2016

I refuse to call Trump racist or sexist, because that wouldn't be politically correct. Instead…

I think it's interesting that a 1990 *Vanity Fair* profile reported Ivana Trump saying that Donald kept a book of Hitler's speeches by his bedside. I have no idea what to make of that or how it represents the man, but some people might find that interesting. There are also a couple of personal anecdotes that might be of interest — so lets get them out of the way.

On my season of *The Apprentice,* the winning "Project Manager" was able to "advise" Trump while sitting next to him in the Boardroom. On my second stint doing this, things took an unexpected turn when he grew quite angry when a contestant self-effacingly referred to himself as "white trash." Trump, apparently disgusted, snapped and "fired" him on the spot. Was this Trump spotting an opportunity to surprise the audience and feigning disgust, was Trump trying to show that he had no tolerance for any kind of racial statements, or was Trump personally offended that someone would dare use a demeaning term towards the white race? White Pride websites cheered "Trump's reaction to the anti-White term" and saw his strong reaction as a little-seen-but-much-needed defense from the constant attacks on whites.[1] I'm not sure what it was, but I still find the whole thing kind of weird.

Another anecdote worth mentioning came early in the show's filming on a visit to the Playboy Mansion. Meeting Hugh Hefner and spending some time with Trump was the reward for winning our weekly task. For context: Including me, my team had consisted of seven women and two men. We started the evening being greeted at the door by Hefner's three girlfriends before we got to have a little fireside chat with him. Trump and a group of playmates then joined us as we adjourned to the Mansions' grounds for a cocktail party. It was shortly after Trump's arrival that I found myself in a conversation circle with him, Hefner, and another contestant. With a wry smile, Trump looked at Hefner and said, "It's hard to tell which of these girls are yours, and which ones are mine." Implying that he saw all of the women in attendance – the incredibly educated and credentialed female business professionals who were applying to work for him *and* the scantily clad Playmates, alike – as the same. While not the most sexist comment I'd ever heard, that it was uttered so casually, with a smirk, left an impression. Afterwards, I chatted about the moment with another contestant and she rolled her eyes and said something to the effect of "what else do you expect from him?" Considering that, while running for president he may have[2] implied that Fox News reporter, Megyn Kelly, who had engaged him in a critical back-and-forth, was menstruating, this hardly qualifies as his most provocative statement.

Those personal anecdotes are fun to write, but I won't dwell in these types of things in the rest of the book. They are basically distractions to the much larger, and more interesting, questions raised by Trump's ascendancy. It is important to understand the man, so I'll share stories and opinions of him where it pertains to his motives, his policies, and potential governing style, but not the (very easy) potshots that I could take. I'll save those for when he attacks this book and me.

The failure of Trump's detractors to understand his *appeal* and the failure of his supporters to understand *him* have produced this remarkable moment. As plainly as I can, I will share my take on the current context in America that's fueled Trump's rise and intersperse that with my firsthand knowledge of Trump, reality TV, the political process, the media, marketing, the evolution of the Republican Party and an overview of the nation's economic & security situations to decode The Donald.

REPUBLICAN RECKONING

I ran for Congress in 2010, an election remarkable because it birthed the "Tea Party wave." In the aftermath of a heralded 2008 election that was supposed to usher in a new era of bipartisan cooperation, 2010, instead, revealed that extreme partisanship was as severe as ever. The two political parties descended into an all out war driven by elected officials who feared being punished by their base for independent thinking. Ideological purity was in. I now see 2010 as just the sneak peak of what's unfolding in the 2016 Republican presidential primary.

In 2015, Michael Lind penned an insightful article for *Politico*, highlighting the puzzle at the core of the Republican Party.[3] Lind explained that the reason a band of misfits seemed to keep rising up in the Republican primaries was not a mystery, but the logical result of past events. Lind laid out how the modern Republican Party actually consists of three separate movements: libertarianism, neo-conservativism, and the religious right. An always uneasy alliance, it was now yielding curious results.

Libertarians want to massively shrink government (eliminate Medicare, social security, and most agencies, to get the government out and let markets work); Neoconservatives want to massively increase military spending to actively police the world (intervene in foreign wars to remake the world with our interests in mind); The so-called "religious right" want to mingle Christian values and directives into US government policy (criminalizing abortion, banning gay marriage, reinstating prayer in schools, etc).

The challenges are obvious: How do you fuse these disparate movements into a coherent ideology to govern? How do you reconcile the contradictory clashes between the groups to maintain peace? A government using religious doctrine to intervene in private lives probably wouldn't thrill libertarians. Neoconservatives probably don't have their hearts warmed by the libertarian desire to "starve the beast" of the military industrial complex.

The believers of all three movements are the core of the party and are the ones who show up to vote in the primaries. They care more about their ideology than they do about party unity or such things. This has caused primary participants to adopt a variety of increasingly extreme and incongruous positions that look much less like the Republican Party of even fifteen years ago.

Part of the inexplicability of Trump's ascendancy was that he subverted the traditional path in a primary for a *fringe* candidate. Traditionally, non-mainstream candidates pick one of these three pillars to form the base of their support. Think: Mike Huckabee and the Religious Right or Ron Paul and Libertarians. Interestingly, Trump's managed another trick:

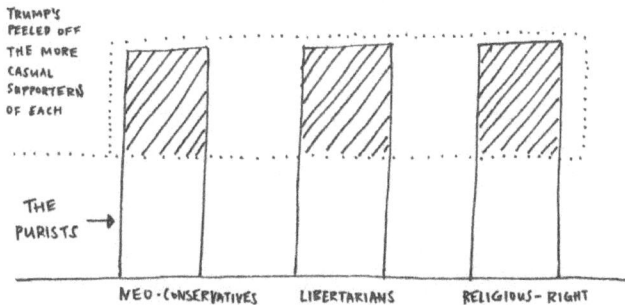

TRUMP'S PEELED OFF THE MORE CASUAL SUPPORTERS OF EACH

THE PURISTS →

NEO-CONSERVATIVES   LIBERTARIANS   RELIGIOUS-RIGHT

The common thread of all three pillars is anxiety and dissatisfaction with the status quo. Neo-conservatives are upset about the loss of our influence and long to return to the days of American hegemony. Libertarians are upset at the government's heavy encroachment into everyday life and long to return to the pioneer days of America's no/low-government founding. The Religious Right is upset with an amoral society and longs to return to a more homogenous rule under Christian moral values. All three speak to a desire for purity. Trump has appealed across all three with his populist messaging and dog-whistles to returning America to yesteryear. He seems to attract the most criticism from the true believers of the three movements and draws his supporters from the more casual sympathizers within.

A group Trump has been feuding with has been Fox News. When Fox first emerged in the mid-90's, it seemed as if Christmas came early for the Republican Party. It was a 24/7 clear, forceful voice for the Republican agenda. Pressing enemies while cheerleading the base, Fox News rocketed to the top of the cable ratings while building a loyal following and powerful brand. Today it's the most lucrative name in news—generating $1 billion in profits.[4]

As such things go, Fox eventually wanted more. Instead of waiting to find out the conservative position from the Republican power brokers, it eventually started to *dictate* the positions. As Fox riled up the base against an issue, elected Republicans were flooded with phone calls and criticism if they weren't aligned with the Fox position. David Frum, George W. Bush's former speechwriter and a once-prominent neoconservative, put it best: "Republicans originally thought that Fox worked for us. Now we're discovering that we work for Fox.[5]"

That all makes it more interesting that Trump has been the first prominent Republican to openly challenge Fox's monopoly on the Republican voice. His casual brand of populism that rejects the orthodoxy of any single faction almost looks like an existential threat to the coalition of acolytes that Fox has amassed. This would also explain why, despite his thrashing of one of their foremost TV personalities, Megyn Kelly, Fox News has done everything it can to make peace with Trump. As only Trump can, he has not relented in trying to bring Fox to heel. The Trump/Fox News clash has been one of the more remarkable things about this election. The relationship soured to the point where Trump boycotted the final debate before the Iowa primary, based on his disagreements with the Fox News moderators.

The Fox News crew is probably downright nostalgic thinking back to the heady days post Obama's inauguration. Obama's election managed to infuriate and unite the holy trinity of the libertarian, neoconservative, religious right base in opposition. Fox News turned into a 24/7 Obama Opposition network and ratings soared. Eventually the collective fury of the base (no doubt aided by Fox's stoking) would give birth to what became known as the "Tea Party." Key Republicans, initially caught off-guard by Obama's energizing of the leftist core to secure his landslide victory, saw the "Tea Party" as *the* opportunity to energize *their* core. Behind the scenes, billionaires like the Koch brothers lavished the fledgling movement with funding for organizational support and PAC-fueled ad spending to give the "grassroots movement" some steroids.

The Tea Party roiled the 2010 mid-term elections, causing one of the largest routs in electoral history (including my Congressional campaign!), converting 60 seats in the House to Republican control. Just two years after Obama's election, the Republicans seemed to have found their counter to Obama's landslide victory. The Republican donors and strategists who had moved quickly to back the movement, looked brilliant. And yet.

"Every revolution carries with it the seeds of its own destruction"
– Frank Herbert, *Dune*

In retrospect, the signs were always there. Candidates, like Todd Akin, would win the Republican primary, and go on to promote brilliant concepts like "legitimate rape," and blow a sure win. Candidates like Akin won their primary because their extreme language and positions endeared them to the Tea Party, but even in solidly Republican states and election cycles, they were too toxic (or stupid?) for the general election. A Delaware Senate candidate even needed to air TV commercials explaining that she wasn't a witch (which didn't seem to help).[6] In all these cases there was much behind-the-scenes hand wringing because tea-party favorites were defeating much more moderate, experienced elected officials in the primary. Yet, the people demanded purity and candidates untainted by the system – and they were willing to lose elections if that was the cost.

As the anxiety of the times spread throughout the country, it bonded with the extreme factions at the core of the Republican Party. Fox News served as the perfect host for that virulent outrage, contempt, and the demands of the base to spread out into the world. Even as some dismissed Fox News' constant coverage of the "Obama as a secret Muslim" storyline as desperate or unhinged,[7] it resonated and spread. In fact, the Congresswoman I ran against had the dubious distinction of being caught on tape as a "birther." Fox also found success with continued, non-stop coverage of The War on Christmas, ISIS, and exposés on how the poor were defrauding the government. Energized by their success (a historic turnover of Congress in 2010) and a newly compliant Congress (Republicans fearing primary challenges, acting as docile kittens to the base) the hodgepodge of factions within the Republican Party, "the base," would no longer stand to be dictated to. The right wing think tanks and best laid plans of billionaires would prove no match for the deep disgust in the hearts of tens of millions of Americans tired of belonging to someone else's Republican Party. It's only in hindsight that Sarah Palin's 2008 ascendancy can be seen not as an anomaly, but a harbinger.

Enter Donald Trump

"We got $18 trillion in debt. We got nothing but problems ... we're dying. We're dying. We need money ... we have losers. We have people that don't have it. We have people that are morally corrupt. We have people that are selling this country down the drain ... the American dream is dead."[8]

Those are fighting words and Trump aims to be our "Wartime President." What, maybe, no one but Trump (and, ironically, Bernie Sanders) saw is that over a hundred million Americans feel under siege. It's not a battle against another country, as much as one for America's soul. While critics mock "Make America Great Again," I think it's brilliant. It cuts right to the heart of Trump's core message:

1. America is getting its ass kicked
2. Things used to be much better
3. Trump can fix this … if you let him

Trump is the people's billionaire. Pick a random Trump profile (from way too many out there) and it won't be long before he's referred to as some variation of the working class idea of a billionaire. Long obsessed with attention and his brand, *The Apprentice* gave Trump the perfect vehicle to project himself as the uncompromising arbiter of good business judgment.

Trump speaks plainly, without delicacy or apology. He admits to having donated money to candidates in exchange for favors, and tells us that he can't be bought. He reminds us constantly that he's a winner (and rich!). He chides us that America's been losing. That last one resonates so well because it's a fresh message that *also* happens to jive with what so many feel in their day-to-day lives. These things make Trump a breath of fresh air and a reputable candidate.

With each passing month, the experts repeatedly screamed that Trump had *finally* gone too far: "He's implying that most Mexican immigrants were criminals! He wants to block Muslims from entering the country! He claims that he'd seen thousands of Muslims in New

Jersey celebrating 9/11!" Each attack against these statements only strengthened the resolve of his supporters. Like them, Trump was tough. He wouldn't apologize or back down like all the other politicians. Trump was, indeed, *different*.

I planned on explaining the inexplicability of Trump's rise by likening him to a 'confidence man.' Like Sawyer on *LOST*, a con(fidence) man uses trickery to find his way into a victim's confidence before ripping them off. As I was building the case for this, I found an even more apt analogy: Trump's rise is best explained along the lines of a religious founder.

The concept of a "religious genius" refers to someone with the unique skillset to capture the imaginations of the masses, convert that into support & devotion, and then create a structure that will outlive them. I'm skeptical that "Trumpism" will outlast the man, but this archetype is the best model I've found for the Trump phenomenon.

I say this because most of Trump's plans and explanations for his positions seem to boil down to "trust me."

How will President Trump get Mexico to *pay* for construction of a 2,000-mile wall to staunch the flow of illegal immigrants and secure our border? *Trust him.* How will President Trump get China to stop the mercantilist policies that have devastated the US manufacturing base? Since much of the damage has already been inflicted and with China's transition to a market economy, how will he heal past harm? *Trust him.* How will President Trump fix a Veterans Affairs department that has struggled to provide the healthcare and other services for millions of at-risk veterans? *Trust him.* How will President Trump cut the head off of ISIS and then take their oil, to boot? *Trust him.*

These declarations require a suspension of disbelief. They require blind faith and devotion, the same that we give our deities. So here—in this moment of national insecurity, pressing challenges, and bizarre political theater—is Trump to tell us that everything will be okay. He's here to fix everything and all that is required of us is our devotion and ignorance of anything that contradicts him. His approach is like the "laying on of hands," the practice whereby religious prophets and faith healers cure various debilitating ailments by just touching the afflicted.

Mexicans or Chinese taking our jobs? *Layeth on the hands!*
Muslim extremists threatening America? *Layeth on the hands!*
Scarily mounting national debt? *Layeth on the hands!*

"They're bringing drugs. They're bringing crime. They're rapists. And some, I assume, are good people." With those gems about Mexican immigrants, Trump jumped into the lead. Always the master of performance, Trump stoked a clear "us versus them" divide. Recently he's moved on from Mexicans and focused on Muslims. Whether American or foreign, he's discussed blanket bans, national registries, and demonized refugees that have fled for their lives. Anger is powerful and Trump's the master of channeling it. Trump wants the *fight* taken to anyone who stands in his way—Democrats, primary opponents, or even the Republican Party itself, if need be. Trump has made clear repeatedly that he'll run as an Independent if there are those who would stand in his way.

There *is* a large amount of existential uncertainty out there, the high-level details of which are covered in the next chapter. Suffice it to say for now, the problems we face are very complicated—it's always the things we can't wrap our brains around, the really complicated problems, that are the scariest. It's hard to know where to even start and that makes us feel powerless. At times like these, I think we're especially willing to believe anyone who tells us they know what to do. Imagine being lost in an unfamiliar place and if, after months of feeling hopelessly lost, you came across someone who, with great confidence, tells you they know exactly where you are and how to get back to safety. What would you do? Every fiber of my being would want to reach toward this person with full trust. You're drowning, alone and out at sea, and someone throws you a life preserver. Would you argue?

Additionally, much of this is self-inflicted. The Trump chicken now coming home to roost was hatched when Republican leadership demonized Obamacare, disingenuously promised to repeal it, and then ground Washington policy-making to a halt.

Back in the early 1990's the Clinton administration tried to pass a comprehensive healthcare reform bill, which a Republican-led effort successfully killed. Fifteen years later, with another Democratic president trying again, the Republicans committed themselves to robbing Obama of a signature victory. Pulling out all the stops, their campaign against it promised job losses, small business closures, massive price increases, and even, courtesy of Sarah Palin, death panels. With Democratic control over the Senate and House of Representatives, the Health Care reform (called The Affordable Care Act, a.k.a. Obamacare) passed in 2010. Even though all involved knew the bill's passage was pretty much inevitable, demonizing the "government takeover of healthcare" served as a rallying cry and allowed Republicans to inflame the base.

Throughout my campaign in 2010, the bill and the anger it stoked were palpable. My opponent,

Congresswoman Jean Schmidt, and basically every other Republican candidate for office, promised to repeal the bill if (re)-elected. That obviously didn't happen. As five years and counting have now passed, a repeal is practically impossible, mainly because the popular parts of the bill (discussed in *The Art of the Bankruptcy*)—like allowing dependents to stay on their parents insurance until age 26, ending rescission, and ending denial of coverage based on pre-existing conditions—would be removed as part of the process. Since it's almost impossible to take benefits away from people, this would be akin to political suicide.[10] The only realistic path would be to keep the things people liked, but remove the taxes and mandates that pay for the popular provisions. Obviously, that would significantly add to the debt, so this seems unlikely. Less interesting, there's also debate if it's even legislatively *possible* to repeal the bill using wonky procedures like reconciliation.[11] All of this means that the Republican Party's strategy of using this as a "wedge" issue to fire up the base, demonize Democrats, and win elections (which, by the way, worked) ended up arousing the anger of their base without any payoff or release. File it under "be careful what you wish for," since that anger has grown.

In the shadow of this, Washington has ground to a halt. With Senate Leader Mitch McConnell promising that his number one priority would be to make Obama a one-term president,[12] Congress approved such a small amount of legislation that it has neared levels not seen since the 1940s.[13] Back then, this sort of Washington inaction spurred President Harry Truman to coin the nickname "The Do Nothing Congress." While deindustrialization ripped apart communities and other ills made every day life harder to manage, Washington seemed apathetic, clueless, and not up to the task.

Into this atmosphere of deep discontent, Trump appeared as an antidote for those who were beyond fed up with failed politicians who looked and sounded the same (Another Bush or Clinton, *anyone?*). He can't be accused of sounding like a politician. He's taken bold, defiant stances on issues and with the same confidence that he proclaims his fabulous wealth and success, he's promised to make America great again. I guess I'm less *surprised* by his success, than I am by the mainstream's reaction to his success. The reasons for The Donald's rise have been in front of us this entire time, starting with the reckoning within his own Republican Party.

NATIONAL INSECURITY

Trump's campaigning is aggressive and borderline angry. His bold positions on Mexican and Muslim immigration, as well as confronting China, resonate deeply with a large chunk of the American people. I believe that's the result of successfully tapping into the newest vein of American insecurity.

The prospect of an attack on American soil seemed unfathomable before September 11th. Its wake brought a literal insecurity, a fear for the continuance of domestic safety. While Europe and the rest of the world need only look to recent memory of what a war in the domestic homeland can unleash, America can not. While London was shelled in WWII, Americans not directly fighting, watched it on the news. The almost fifteen years since the 9/11 attacks reveal a nation still uncomfortable and adjusting to an everyday uncertainty.

Trump has masterfully hit popular opinion by characterizing the Bush years as foolish, dangerous over-reaction and blasting the current Obama-years as naive, dangerous under-reaction. It's with that lens that we get Trump's calls for a blanket ban on Muslims entering the US, interest in a national registry for domestic Muslims, and his denouncements of 'W's" unpopular war in Iraq.

In retrospect, 2001 was also notable because it marked the start of a dramatic transition of power in our relationship with China. As our national budget spiraled upward, it required enormous debt to fund large tax cuts and the increased military spending for Middle East wars. As the Chinese economy roared forward behind exports to the US, produced by its rapidly growing manufacturing base, China was flush with excess American dollars. The Chinese government then used these dollars to buy up the debt we were selling. As the largest holder of US debt,[14] China is our largest creditor and makes up almost half of our massive $700 billion annual trade deficit.[15] Given all this, it makes sense that Trump's loud attacks against the Chinese for taking advantage of our *stupid* leaders and stealing *our* jobs have found an eager audience.

Like a master bartender, Trump seamlessly blends America's physical and economic insecurities into a perfect cocktail. As America has grown less white, and imports dominate store shelves, Trump has found a captive, eager audience and provided them with villains. That Trump chose to demonize Mexican immigrants as rapists and criminals seemed like a curious choice to many. Why, with so many more pressing issues—from debt, unemployment, or terrorism—is he obsessed with building a wall?

What Trump saw was that Mexican immigration spoke to a larger anxiety about foreign influence. Trump's non-politically correct solution ("Build a damn wall to keep the criminals out!") appealed to a growing population of people who feared that their country was too quickly changing in too many ways they didn't like. Sure, he was talking about a wall, but it might as well have been a time machine.

Economic Insecurity: A Foreign Landscape

When my parents grew up in the 1950's in small villages in India, America was spoken about with a mythical reverence as a country of beauty, abundance, and security. For millions, my parents included, that's still their frozen-in-time snapshot of an idealized America. This America, in the aftermath of World War II, is also the one that Trump calls back to when he promises to make us great again.

As WWII ended and soldiers returned home, factories roared to life. As a result of the war, worldwide infrastructure—roads, factories, schools, airports, etc—were in ruins and American goods were the only game in town. Even with this basic monopoly on supply, the most powerful source of demand came from American consumers. As factories hummed, record numbers of homes and the great Interstate Highway System were built. A vast shared prosperity transformed the nation. The booming middle class, with the Great Depression and the sacrifices of WWII behind them, were finally able to spend their wages on building secure lives. This kicked off a virtuous cycle where that spending fueled greater demand for factory-produced goods, which led to higher wages and so on.

What altered the post-WWII reality were technological advancements. Throughout history, these advancements have constantly changed the lives of workers and the nature of economies. Starting in the 1980's, that technology took the form of turbo-charging the effectiveness of automation and, along with it, globalization.

Automation—whether in the form of a sewing machine, computer, or gigantic robotic arms that assemble cars—helps factories produce way more per employee.[16] Factories require fewer workers to make more goods. While there's much more noise about globalization (next paragraph), it's estimated that more American jobs have been lost to automation and technology-driven efficiency gains than to foreign workers.[17]

Despite the best efforts of the *Terminator* movies, sinister robots on assembly lines are not a nightmare visual for most Americans. The sight of American factories shuttering as production moved overseas proved far scarier. While American consumers continued to purchase the same items, our purchases now supported the jobs of foreign workers, whereas that might once have been our neighbor's job. Ironically, because formerly middle-class Americans (impacted by job losses) had less disposable income, they ended up being drawn to the cheaper products from overseas, continuing the vicious cycle.

Job exportation and automation-led efficiency gains together were quite the gut punch for the American worker. America's national love affair with "free-markets" basically encouraged companies to maximize short-term profits to send jobs abroad. Meanwhile, the government's main contributions seemed to be a tangle of ill-designed regulations and taxes that only increased companies' desire to move toward foreign labor.

Our de facto national policy has been: "You want to move those jobs to China? Go for it! We probably shouldn't make that anyway." This led to one of the great distortions in American history, the right-but-wrong idea that in free trade, everyone wins. To this day, the majority of very smart folks accept the absolute good of free trade as a fundamental truth as if a non-interventionist, free-market approach to economics and trade was a bedrock founding principle of American economics, which is ironic, because the truth is closer to the opposite.

Alexander Hamilton, America's first Treasury Secretary, was a genius (that duel with Aaron Burr, aside). Hamilton was such an impressive man, all these years later he's honored by a wildly popular Broadway musical that is impossible to get tickets for (*Help me, Lin Manuel. You're my only hope*). Anyway, shortly after we defeated the British and secured American independence, Hamilton produced a report for Congress called *The Report on Manufactures*. It advocated the buildup of domestic manufacturing to give our economy a solid foundation for *economic* independence. We had just won a war to gain our literal freedom and he feared that dependence on foreign nations would eventually threaten our economic freedom. He feared a tyranny through other means.

Hamilton's plan recommended that America build its industrial base through subsidies to industry, tariffs on imports, and other forms of government support.[18] While these policies were debated for years and not fully implemented until Lincoln's presidency, they were a key part of our nation's rise and formed the basis of what became known as the "American School" of economics.

American School policies helped infant American industries using incentives funded by tariffs on imports. Visiting scholars from Germany and Japan loved the idea and brought these lessons back to their native lands. By the beginning of the 20th century, Germany, Japan and the US had all nearly caught up to the British Empire in economic might, which was fitting, since Britain had used similar policies to build up its own industries.

After WWII, with all other major world economies severely crippled from battle (especially the once globally dominant German and Japanese producers), the US found itself as the last nation standing. With not a single economic competitor in sight, we began the long process of relaxing our competitive instincts. This culminated in our current entrenched mindset that America can't lose from "free trade" and that our workers will always prevail.

This overconfidence ignored the reasons for our dominance: the reality of America's post-WWII accidental killer-advantage, as well as the economic policies that built up the employment and manufacturing base in the first place.

New competition from imports started becoming a noticeable part of the American economy in the '70s and '80s. Faced with competition from low-cost foreign imports and the pressure to increase profits, companies reacted by moving production overseas to create cost savings. Advances in transportation, communication, and the proliferation of low-cost computing in the workplace made managing foreign supply chains very doable. Fueled by automation and globalization, the manufacturing jobs that were the backbone of the middle class began to wither.

The modern era truly kicked off on December 8, 1993 when President Bill Clinton signed the North American Free Trade Agreement (NAFTA) into law. The bill removed trade barriers in the Canada-US-Mexico market to a freer flow of goods. Martinsville, Virginia, a region known first for tobacco production, and then furniture making, was an area that soon felt the impact. In 1998, Martinsville had an unemployment rate of 15.2%, at a time when the national average was 4.2%.[19] During the post-WWII golden age, unemployment in Martinsville was less than 1%.

In 2001, China joined the World Trade Organization (WTO), which made it a member of the body that governed international trade. This foreshadowed the hollowing out of the American manufacturing base and a dramatic shift in the nature of that post-WWII "middle class" life. As jobs went overseas, millions of Americans' wages stagnated and their lives diverged from their former middle-class existence. It was an unsettling "new normal" for many. From 2001 to 2012, over 63,000 American factories closed while China's manufacturing sector added over 14 million jobs.[20]

That's the backdrop for the first act in our play, which takes place in the last few years of the '90s and the early part of the 2000s. The stock market had soared thanks to technology stocks, with companies like pets.com being valued in the billions, despite losing unbelievable amounts of money. As required in all bubbles, it was accepted that the party would never end with stock prices increasing forever. The stories were plentiful of someone without investing experience making a killing in the stock market. Trillions of dollars in wealth were created out of thin air and filled the pockets of millions of Americans. Stock market gains were used to supplement income and, more importantly, helped support our consumer-led economy by fueling consumer spending.

When the dot-com bubble imploded, it took much of the stock market's gains with it. With trillions of dollars wiped out in a matter of weeks, it drove the economy into a serious recession. Central bankers, led by Federal Reserve Chairman Alan Greenspan, tried to improve things by cutting interest rates to record lows, which ignited act two.

Greenspan's actions translated into record-low mortgage interest rates. Low mortgage rates translated to very low monthly mortgage payments, which set off a massive housing boom. This meant renters could now save money each month by buying a home, and those who already owned homes, could now afford a more expensive one. Everyone was buying!

These factors created our next bubble. With a home buying frenzy underway, prices began increasing as buyers competed for limited housing inventory. Soon, it looked like housing prices could only go up, and it wasn't uncommon to see yearly double-digit percentage increases. The insanity took on a life of its own from there. Thanks to new financial inventions like debt securitization,[21] banks stopped verifying borrower income information (NINJA loans: No Income, No Job/Assets ... loans!) and rampant speculation followed, which set off a massive construction boom. Meanwhile, whether by selling a home for a nice profit or borrowing money against the increase in a home's value, Americans had a new piggybank to tap for spending money. As in the dot-com bubble, this extra money helped people forget about their newly shrunken incomes. They went back to supporting our consumer-led economy by spending.

In 2008, like the dot.com bubble, our new housing bubble *also* imploded. As housing prices collapsed, America learned that banks had used the housing boom as an opportunity to basically turn themselves into casinos. In effect, the banks used financial instruments to make a massive, *massive* bet that housing prices would never go down. When the banks learned that they had just lost every single bet, they were essentially insolvent. The government felt compelled to step in and covered the bets by taking over trillions of dollars in bank losses to prevent a global depression.

For our purposes, whether the banks' actions were massive financial fraud or a terrible accident is irrelevant, because the net impact is what we're focused on: Trillions of dollars were once again wiped out in a matter of weeks and, once again, spending sharply decreased, sending the economy into a recession from which it still has not truly recovered.

Throughout these bubbles, credit was the consistent American response to a deteriorating financial situation. It's estimated that consumer credit card debt is around $900 billion.[22] Remarkably, more than half of the lower and middle-income Americans who carry balances for longer than three months used credit cards to pay for day-to-day expenses like food and gas.[23] This meant that without access to credit, these folks might not be able to secure basic staples.

This all proved especially distressing, because the slowdown in new home building also happened to hit the highest paying of the newly created middle-class construction jobs. Without a way to spend money they didn't have, consumers shopped less, ate out less, and went on vacation less. This triggered the opposite of the aforementioned post-WWII virtuous cycle. As the economy dipped, people had less money to spend, which led to the closing of restaurants and retail stores, which then cut hours and laid off workers, which meant more people had less money to spend, and so it went.

The storm had been building for years. The bubbles and cheap credit had masked how bad things were. As America lost the high paying manufacturing jobs that served as the backbone of the middle class (which made America great), there were hiccups sustaining a primarily consumption-driven economy. It turns out that without a broad base of people who actually have jobs and money to spend on consumer goods, things get dicey. Since the '08 crisis, the unprecedented action of setting interest rates near 0% helped to jumpstart the economy, but without consumers returning to their shopaholic ways with credit,[24] it's been a delicate recovery at best.

Meanwhile, the divide between the *haves* and the *have-nots* has only grown. The new multi-billion dollar businesses created—such as LinkedIn, Facebook, and Google—are largely technology companies that, unlike manufacturing businesses, don't employ large amounts of people. Facebook, a $318 billion dollar company, employed 12,000 people at the end of 2015.[25] That so much value could be created with so few employees would have been unthinkable just 20 years ago. Those 12,000 employees are essentially all white-collar knowledge workers such as computer programmers, designers, and business types. Whereas once a successful American company could be counted on as a source of solid, blue-collar jobs, this is now the exception.

As blue-collar manufacturing jobs disappeared, retail stores and restaurants—leaders of a consumption driven economy—were the source of new jobs. These were the kinds of jobs that required a physical presence and couldn't be easily outsourced. With the reduction in manufacturing and other higher-paying jobs, the newly unemployed only had these types of opportunities available to them. Deindustrialization, having affected a large enough group of people, meant that the laws of supply and demand anchored wages to the low end. A 2013 MIT study showed that "for each year low-wage American factory workers were exposed to competition from Chinese goods, their wages fell 2.6% more than higher-wage factory workers'."[26] In other words, our new jobs didn't pay very well.

Meanwhile, those at the high-end of the labor force benefited tremendously from these dual forces. Thanks to automation, a shift to overseas production, and now cheaper American labor, there were sharp decreases in production costs. Nations like China, which benefited from the shifting of jobs, also produced hundreds of millions of new consumers to buy American products, which meant increased corporate revenues. While decreased costs and increased revenues meant record corporate profits for American companies, it also divorced the fate of the American worker, no longer making that American company's products, from the success of her (probably former) company. The result was that, from 1996-2011, corporate profits were up 106%, which has helped drive the S&P stock index up 141%. Worker pay saw a 4.3% increase while senior executive pay increased 298%.[27] More recently, these benefits continued to pile up as the historically low interest rates were used for corporate borrowing to fund dividends and stock buybacks. The confluence of these factors have all fueled large gains in the stock market, while the bulk of American workers faced anxiety and uncertainty.

For a long while, credit masked the pain and helped to stave off the hangover. Whether in the form of stock/housing market gains or credit cards, these piggy banks helped Americans ignore a painful new reality. Credit let us pretend the post-WWII party had never stopped. No one worried and we just tried to have a good time, but now the party is over and we're all living with the huge hangover. Between 2000 and 2012, three times as many people are now on food stamps.[28]

There is no instant cure for a hangover, nor is there an instant way to fix the middle class employment crisis. As we'll talk about next, we need to return to policies that increase labor flexibility, incentivize businesses to locate jobs here, and enforce trade policies that protect American workers. As we slowly rebuild our middle class jobs, the resulting consumer spending would help spur the needed positive cycle of job creation.

While this all sounds familiar, the degree to which this has impacted the lives of millions of Americans is little appreciated. When Trump blames Mexicans for stealing American jobs and creating economic insecurity, he understands the peace it grants to have a simple culprit to build a wall around. When Ted Cruz creates a brilliant commercial implying that, if the evil Mexicans were stealing white-collar instead of blue-collar jobs, those in power would react far differently, he's tapping that same vein.[29]

Of all the Republican candidates, Trump has focused the most on China.[30] His message is simple: Weak American leaders allowed China to steal *your* job and make *you* poorer. The label on the back of so many imports perfectly encapsulates the alienation and anger that many detect in the Trump movement. I call it *Hecho en China.*

The fact that things in America are not written only in English compounds the growing alienation many feel in a dramatically changing country. When the label, Made in China appears on an item an American might have once made, it fuels an anger that things have gone terribly wrong and we're heading in the wrong direction. To me, *Hecho en China* is shorthand for today's world where American workers feel abandoned by their government, countries like China have "stolen" their jobs, and they feel marginalized in their own country. They begin to think, *I have to read about how another country has taken my job in another language!* I've alluded to the fact that moving American jobs offshore is at the core of many of our issues and, since China is the poster child of this, let's do a quick pass at how this all came to be.

Cheap Labor

China and other developing countries' workers get paid a lot less than Americans. Decades ago, a still-developing China didn't have enough industry to fully employ their populations, which meant really low wages. Additionally, many countries had an additional supply of labor in the form of children and that further depressed wages. Either way, labor wages always start out cheap and, as economies mature, increase.

Government Subsidies

The Chinese government basically gave free, or substantially discounted land, buildings, energy, and raw materials to domestic companies. China bet that the benefit from new jobs, new industry, and skilled workers would justify its investment in subsidies. Over time, as the government gained confidence that the production had become secure, they ended the subsidies for that industry and moved on to new ones.

Currency Help

Chinese currency manipulation is a favorite political talking point. When China is accused of undervaluing its currency, we think they're doing it so they can export their goods at an artificially low price. The tradeoff is that Chinese citizens have to pay more for imported goods. So China is incentivizing its people to save and its industries to produce. The effect for us is the opposite. American exports cost more for Chinese consumers, while imported Chinese products are cheaper for Americans. This rewards Chinese producers (with more profits & jobs) while punishing American producers (with fewer profits & jobs). China has been adjusting the value of its currency and, today, many feel that Chinese currency has reached near fair value.[31] Though, with the Chinese economy in pretty rocky shape lately,[32] there's definite concern that they'll devalue it even more, returning us to the problems we had years ago.

Regulatory Environment

Not all low-cost labor factories are alike. Just the cost of complying with American regulations governing factory conditions can be more than the *total* cost of foreign workers' wages. Worker safety protections, number of hours per shift, and environmental conditions vary drastically around the globe. The savings from having a factory's workers handling chemicals without proper equipment, working 12-hour shifts, or directly releasing chemical waste into a nearby river can easily dwarf the cost of wages. Are you ever curious about how that toy could cost just $5 despite being shipped halfway around the world?

Who Pays?

American companies pay for worker healthcare, into social security, for disability insurance, and other employee benefits. As discussed in greater detail in the next chapter, almost every other developed nation has a consumption tax that is used to help pay for their companies' employee benefits.

This is such a crucial concept, let me give you an example: when Cadillac manufactures a CTS-V in Detroit, they spend money on the car's materials, the cost of the factory, wages, health insurance and other regulatory taxes. Cadillac wants to increase sales and intends to sell this car in Germany to the massive, untapped market of Germans who are tired of pretty BMWs and want an American muscle car instead. Let's pretend that Cadillac wants to sell the CTS-V for 100,000 Euros. Germany has a VAT (Value Added Tax, basically a kind of national sales tax) of about 20%, so it'll cost the German consumer 120,000 Euros to own the car with 20,000 Euros going to the German government.

The German government will then use part of this VAT revenue to help pay for their public services; e.g. the German public healthcare system. This means the cost of a car made in America, but sold in Germany, contains all its raw product costs, *plus* the health insurance of the autoworkers in Detroit who made the car, *plus* the healthcare of the German who bought the car (through their VAT). This is why anything made in America exported to a country with a VAT is at a cost disadvantage. The options for that company are to move their jobs to a country where they can take advantage of a VAT to lower their labor costs, or to struggle selling to that market at a significant price disadvantage.

Market Access

When a Chinese factory wants to export to America they can basically just set up shop. On the other hand, if an American company wants to sell to China's 1.4 billion consumers, it had better be prepared to negotiate.[33] If that company makes something the Chinese government wants its companies to eventually produce, it'll be asked for two things. As an example, let's stick with cars and General Motors (maker of Cadillac).[34]

The first thing China will ask the American company to do is form a joint venture with a local Chinese firm. In 1997, GM went halfsies (50/50) with SAIC, a Chinese company that had little experience building world-class automobiles.[35] Since then, GM has become the largest foreign automaker in China, and SAIC has become a world-class player in auto design, engineering, and manufacturing. While GM would prefer to own 100% of their China business, without a local partner they couldn't even *sell* in China.

The second thing China will ask for is a "technology transfer." The government's goal in requiring GM to form a joint venture with a local player like SAIC is to improve the local company's knowledge and capabilities. GM had to share key R&D and technological advances with SAIC to help them "catch up." The risk, of course, is that GM is helping to create a formidable competitor—not only in China, but also worldwide.

The tightrope is clear: While an American company wants to grow its business and needs access to the world's biggest market to do it, such short-term needs clash with the long-term danger of creating a competitor.

Linkages

When China lures production overseas, it gets more than just *those* jobs. As Clyde Prestowitz, Secretary of Commerce under President Reagan, frequently points out, there are strong linkages between manufacturing, R&D, education, and economies of scale.[36] It's through these linkages that Apple has shifted, not just its manufacturing, but also its entire supply chain to China.[37] The need for quick prototyping and an immediate supply of parts—from tiny screws to microchips—led Apple to locate production in China's Shenzen province, which produces the majority of the world's phones. That meant that within miles, Apple had everything it needed and it became increasingly complicated for parts to come from anywhere else.

That's how spending whatever it takes to kick-start a new industry can end with owning an entire process and the jobs that come with it. When American factories move overseas, a key consideration is a foreign country's steady source of well-trained workers. When enough companies operate in a similar industry, it's economical to provide the educational programs to provide industry-specific worker training. Recently as Chinese labor costs have gone up, along with rising fears of intellectual property theft, some American companies have looked to bring production home—only to find they no longer had access to workers with the proper training to operate the factories.[38]

Again, China didn't invent the model of leveraging these strategies to build up their jobs base. We followed this playbook for over a century with spectacular results and, before us, the British Empire did. However, as maybe only an autocratic dictatorship can, China took it to another level.

Trump likes to remind everyone that China found the perfect partner in American leaders. As a nation of consumers, we valued cheaper prices above all else. With China's help, our leaders delivered. It's the reason for China's unprecedented ascent in wealth, exports, education, and production capabilities. While our ignorance is on display in our own string of unprecedented records—record trade deficits, record foreign control of our government debt, and income inequality not seen since the 1920s.

It takes willful blindness to ignore that the factors behind China's rise also helped rebuild Germany and Japan after WWII and were used pre-WWII to setup America's golden age. The only path to more manufacturing jobs are policies sharply focused on helping domestic companies become globally competitive. The factors laid out in this chapter and their implications for jobs and where manufacturing goes, must be acknowledged and incorporated into public policy. This will be good not only for America, but also the world. "China makes; the world takes," is not sustainable forever.[39] It's not as incendiary as abortion, gay marriage, or who to bomb next—the issues that easily divide Americans—but it's crucial.

The global war for jobs isn't new, as it goes back prior to the founding of America. For over a century, we supported our companies and our workers and, in the process, built a thriving economy. We fought to win. At peak strength, (perhaps blinded by hubris?) we decided we no longer needed to fight for jobs and essentially became economic pacifists. Other nations continued to fight and, in the process, began dominating the battle on behalf of their domestic workers.

It's hard, if not impossible, for a company to fight a foreign government. Ideally governments shouldn't get involved in private sector matters, such as where a company locates a factory. They should let the free-market work and companies should settle their own disputes, but when nations begin strongly intervening on behalf of their domestic companies, it's necessary for the other country to also get involved.

So, I'm not blaming the Chinese government. I blame *our* government for turning a blind eye and essentially abandoning American companies and their workers. Anyone who watched Trump's feud with Rosie O'Donnell, knows that he's pretty much a playground bully. For the millions who feel like the Chinese government has acted unfairly, this image of Trump standing up for the American worker actually sounds pretty good. Maybe no one likes a bully, until he's your bully?

∞β∞

I was visiting family in Virginia in early 2012, when I stumbled upon a fascinating window into the China trade wars in *The Roanoke Times*, their local paper. Beth Macy wrote a well-researched series of articles about John Bassett, an American furniture maker and his struggle to keep his plants open[40]. It put a human face on American manufacturing's struggle for survival. Since then, Macy has expanded the articles into a fantastic book: *Factory Man*. It's an incredibly immersive read into the life of the Bassett family, a terrific glimpse into life in manufacturing towns through the decades, and has tons of great family

& trade drama. I tore through it as I was writing this and I couldn't recommend it more as an engrossing guide to the trade wars.

∞β∞

PHYSICAL INSECURITY

I campaigned in a Congressional district that consisted of some very large rural counties. That experience helped give sterile economic statistics—like five million-plus manufacturing jobs lost overseas—real meaning, because so many of those lost jobs were in rural America. Unfortunately, unlike in large cities with a diversity of industry that can give families a chance to start over, most small towns never recovered after the factories closed.

Since I grew up something of a city boy, my time spent out in Appalachian Ohio was a powerful learning experience. While I remember a handful of the new expressions I learned, none stuck with me quite like "us little people." I took it as a colloquial phrase meant to refer to blue-collar workers. There were fancy white-collar types—business owners, lawyers and doctors—and then there were *the little people*. As business after business rushed to boost the bottom line by shuttering factories to move production overseas and lay off longtime workers in the process, I've given that phrase a second look. They weren't being self-effacing by referring to themselves as "little people"—but clearly understood that this was how they were viewed *by* the powerful elites. How else can the matter-of-factness with which economists, politicians, and executives concluded that it would be better for everyone to shutter thousands of factories be explained?

The consequences for tens of millions of families, meant upending a way of life, *their* way of life, which had existed for generations.

As communities unraveled and millions lost their sense of control over their economic destiny, there were twenty-four hour news cycles detailing a never-ending stream of threats. Despite one-thousand times fewer American deaths from terrorism than those killed in gun violence,[41] the news, analysts, and political chatter, all focus on foreign terrorism.

Trump supporters seem especially receptive to extreme statements about terrorism and foreign threats. The base of Trump's support in the primaries comes from the white, blue-collar workers most impacted by recent job losses that threaten their economic security.[42] Anecdotally, it makes sense that those with well-paying jobs, a secure home, and not overly worried about an ability to make ends meet, are also less likely to obsess over the amorphous security threats that might be out there. It's in this vortex of threats, foreign attacks, and domestic insecurity that Trump has found his main opening. He hasn't wasted this opportunity and has lobbed some gems:

- "...total and complete shutdown of Muslims entering the United States until our country's representatives can figure out what is going on."
- *Reporter*: Should there be database that tracks the Muslims that are in this country?
  Trump: There should be a lot of systems, beyond databases. We should have a lot of systems and today you can do it.

- "They're bringing drugs. They're bringing crime. They're rapists. And some, I assume, are good people." *(the "they" being Mexicans)*
- "Cut the head off ISIS and take their oil."

While those statements polarized the general public, Trump's base gobbled it up and sent him to the top of the polls. The media, political pundits, and liberals have been horrified *and* consistently sure that *this* time Trump had *finally* gone *too* far. Nope.

I thought of my campaign and the folks I met who had a tenuous grasp on their economic future and believed that the powerful would always choose making that extra cent of profit over looking out for the "little people." It rang true because it's something I've also heard from my mother. She grew up in a small village in India before working for over twenty years on the mail sorting conveyer line at the United States Postal Service. The life I live couldn't be more different than hers and that sticks with me. I see this reflected in how concerned she gets by the stuff on the nightly news—the degree to which the threats feel real and closing in. I know helplessness isn't the perfect word, but it's the best I can come up with. While I'm sure she's no Trump fan (my parents are pretty fierce Democrats and considering Trump fired her beloved youngest son on national TV, I'd like to think she's still mad at him for that), I see how his statements capture the mood of the country. While the September 11 attacks were startling and eye opening, the wars in Iraq and Afghanistan might have been more jarring in revealing that, regardless of military might, our ability to impose our desires on the world has limits. Despite leading the world in military spending and spending many trillions in the past few years, it's remarkably easy to feel … insecure.

This is a more nuanced point than the harsh economic reality facing much of America, but I think, in many ways, no less threatening to millions. The nature of war has changed and it certainly raises the question whether we've adequately prepared and reacted to the circumstances.

Despite our secure position as the #1 military spender in the world, spending more than the next seven nations combined, we still face existential threats. Unlike the battle scenes in movies, armies today don't line up on opposite sides of a field and fire until one side wins. America's adversaries hide, use deception, and attack where least expected. The most recent Iraq war saw a slew of car bombs, suicide bombers, and land mines deployed against American forces. In fact, this trend of guerilla style tactics has been the trend since Vietnam. This asymmetric nature of combat is even more extreme because our War on Terror isn't against a nation, but an ideology. The enemy could be anyone, anywhere. In recent years, we've seen America's number one enemy morph from bin Laden, to the Taliban, Saddam Hussein, al-Qaeda, and now ISIS. While both our soldiers and civilians face threats not easily seen, our strength still lies within the trillion-dollar naval fleets, high-tech tanks, fighter jets, and other armaments designed for a traditional, symmetrical war.

Facing these non-traditional threats of unknown origin has led to a massive rise in foreign and domestic surveillance. Wire-tapping and monitoring have proliferated and, while arguably very necessary, the recent Snowden and "Wiki-leaks" don't offer Americans much reassurance about the government's competence. That the highest level of government secrets and spying efforts could be so easily leaked by relatively low-level insiders calls into question just how effective these measures are. While it's theoretically possible that it's better to live in a state of ubiquitous surveillance than one of ever-present danger, this would only be a logical premise if the agencies entrusted with monitoring and safeguarding us are competent. If they can't secure their own intelligence, why should they be trusted to make sense of it, connect the dots to security threats, and coordinate defenses against it?

After September 11 and various attacks around the world, more rigorous security procedures in everyday life became the norm. Yet, when I take my shoes off to pass through airport security or I'm patted down entering a Mets game, I'm undergoing a version of security as theater. As the disinterested and distracted security agent goes through the motions, it's obvious that the logistics of all this defies logic or any serious definition of effectiveness. Recently, the TSA failed in ninety-five percent of security tests: They allowed banned items—weapons and explosives—to pass through in sixty-seven of seventy tests conducted across the nation.[43] In a reality where both our soldiers *and* civilians face risks from unexpected attacks, agencies like the TSA with its $7+ billion dollar budget are not inspiring confidence in their ability to catch threats.

Unlike asymmetric threats, which still involve one or more terrorists physically infiltrating our physical protections, cyber-terrorism requires no physical presence to cause calamitous physical damage. In 2012, word leaked that the US used a computer virus to attack Iran's nuclear program—the first time a cyber attack was used as a legitimate military weapon. Over the past decade there have been numerous reports that US companies, intelligence, and other agencies have been hacked on the orders of other governments. A recent Chinese hack exposed the private information of over five million US government employees.[44] It's believed that this information could be used to help the Chinese government with information-gathering and potential espionage.

Security experts have long warned that we're essentially unprepared for an attack on US satellites, the electric grid, computer servers, utility plants, and basically anything computer-based. It's believed that an attack on our power grid could leave a major US city without power for six months.[45] Given that I begin to panic when my iPhone battery dies, I find this especially scary. The prospect of banks, public utilities, or communication satellites thrown into disarray for an extended period of time is far more real than the plot of the next *Die Hard* movie sequel.

If the prospect of cyber-terrorism is scary because it could be done without a physical presence and seemingly so effortlessly, financial warfare is downright terrifying. We owe China and other countries a lot of money (discussed in the next chapter). There are many concerns with having a national debt of $19 trillion and the largest trade deficit in the history of the world, but the operative word is *dependency*. We're reliant on foreign countries for natural resources, products, and financing our government's operations. This can be dangerous if disagreements ever arise and it's not just a theoretical concern. During the 2008 financial crisis, Russia tried to conspire with China to sell US debt to maximize the damage done to our economy.[46] More recently, there's been concern that China and Russia have been conspiring to weaken the US Dollar's role as the world's reserve currency, traditionally one of America's great advantages[47] that allows us to borrow money at the lowest relative rate in the world. This kind of thing isn't even illegal—it's basically how financial markets work. Preying on the weak to inflict maximum financial harm is the time-tested mechanism of financial markets.[48]

Prior to winning the presidency, Dwight Eisenhower served as a five-star general and the Supreme Commander of Allied Forces in Europe.[49] As a successful military leader and two-term president, he understood the above topic better than anyone. In his farewell address to the nation, he coined the term, "military-industrial complex," and expressed concern about the dangers of massive spending. He warned of the dangers of corruption, with so much money at stake, that a powerful set of interests with its tentacles deep into Washington could eventually co-opt how we plan for and defended our national interests.[50] Whether we're talking outfitting our military or homeland security, we seem best at preparing to fight the previous war.

Into this insecurity Trump saunters in, confidently announcing that he has the answers. Unlike President Eisenhower's farewell address, Trump's solutions don't require understanding nuances about the state of affairs, just that a group is bad and he's going to crush them. Whether it's Mexicans bringing crime, Chinese inheriting our jobs, or Muslims trying to kill us, it matters not: Trump knows how to deal with people like them. To tens of millions of Americans, already economically displaced and feeling vulnerable, this sounds tremendously reassuring.

If the conditions within the Republican Party nourished the soil for the rise of such a variety of extreme candidates, it's this economic and security context that's propelled Trump to the top.

THE ART OF THE BANKRUPTCY

"That is what I could do for the country. We owe $19 trillion. Boy, am I good at solving debt problems. Nobody can solve it like me."[51]
                                                                    – Donald Trump

The Art of the Deal is Trump's bestselling book to date and where he details his keys to success. Unfortunately, it was published in 1987, right before Trump fought off various corporate bankruptcies and doesn't feature advice on how to grapple with overwhelming debt.

Trump's four corporate bankruptcy filings give him the dubious distinction of being a leader in the bankruptcy field for the past few decades.[52] In his first bankruptcy filing in 1991 for the Trump Taj Mahal casino in Atlantic City, he even faced the grisly prospect of *personal* bankruptcy. In the course of running up massive corporate debts, Trump personally guaranteed almost $900 million in debt.[53] Through some truly masterful negotiating—namely promising his creditors that he'd see to it that they'd lose *all* their money if they forced him into personal bankruptcy—he survived. He would later deal with three subsequent corporate bankruptcies, but would always manage to come through it personally unscathed.

Of all Trump's accomplishments, avoiding personal bankruptcy and shepherding his businesses through the bankruptcy processes are probably his most legitimate credentials as a candidate. As we'll explore, America's fiscal health is a lot like that of a Trump business: in dire need of rescue thanks to crushing future payments that can't be covered by projected revenues due to overly-leveraged debt. As the saying should go—there's only one guarantee in life: *debt and taxes.* America's financial situation prompts a lot of hand wringing, but very little understanding. Let's do a flyby to understand how Trump's been able to channel the voice of concern about America's finances.

It all starts with our debt. Each year the government spends more than it collects in tax revenue, we run what's called a budget deficit. Adding these deficits together gives us our national debt. If you're a millennial, you may not even know that back in the late 90s, we actually ran a budget surplus. We collected more money than we spent and it went to paying down the already accumulated national debt. That's now a distant memory. For the past fifteen years we've run huge consecutive deficits and the national debt stands at around $19 trillion. A trillion is pretty much unfathomable, so lets break it down to a family of four's share: $150,000. Not a typo.

What's more, that $19 trillion is just what we've already spent. In the future, we're projected to be on the hook for another $46 trillion dollars for items already promised, but we can't pay for.[54] That means we'll have to borrow or, more accurately, borrow *more.*

The Federal Budget Outlook Summarized:

It's hard to believe, but twenty years ago there was concern that the economy might slow down because we didn't have *enough* debt. We were running surpluses and since economists are masters at making up things to worry about, that was the warning. We've since experienced multiple economic slowdowns, increased military spending behind two of the longest wars in American history, and added trillions of dollars in *new* spending programs, all while *cutting* taxes. In other words, we massively increased spending and then massively cut revenue. Between 2000 and today, the national debt skyrocketed from $5.6 trillion to $19 trillion.[55] For the first 224 years of American history = $5.6 trillion. For the 15 years since = $13 trillion! Oopsies.

Ready for some good news? Sorry, there isn't any. The above numbers were just the monies *already spent*. There's an additional $46 trillion committed to programs we can't pay for through the year 2084. Some $8 trillion of this is a social security shortfall, and the other $38 trillion is in Medicare and Medicaid obligations.[56]

If you're in my demographic, the social security taxes taken out of our paychecks go directly to current retirees. When we retire, the same thing is supposed to happen. Those working at that time pay in, and we'll then collect. Unfortunately things are a bit complicated, since population sizes aren't stable over time. Today, a lot more people pay into social security than collect, which leaves billions of dollars left over annually. Sadly, the folks in Washington have happily been using that extra money to pay for other things, leaving IOUs projected to total about $8 trillion. They could have saved this money instead, so that when the day came when we had fewer workers than retirees, there'd be money, but … nope.

While that $8 trillion sounds problematic, it doesn't look so bad when compared to the *$38 trillion* in healthcare bills for which the government is on the hook.[57]

There are two main reasons that bill is so large. First, there's a simple demographic problem: we had a baby boom and soon there will be a very large population of elderly who will need their Medicare paid for. The real problem, however, is that we have the world's most expensive and inefficient healthcare system.

Our inability to fundamentally reform the healthcare system has exacerbated what should have been a manageable problem. A demographic issue alone is solvable,[58] but when costs consistently and annually rise faster than inflation, it's much tougher. Since this is such an important issue that will probably decide America's fiscal fate, I dissect our healthcare system in slightly greater depth at the end of this chapter.

In the startup world, there's this Holy Grail of a hockey stick graph:

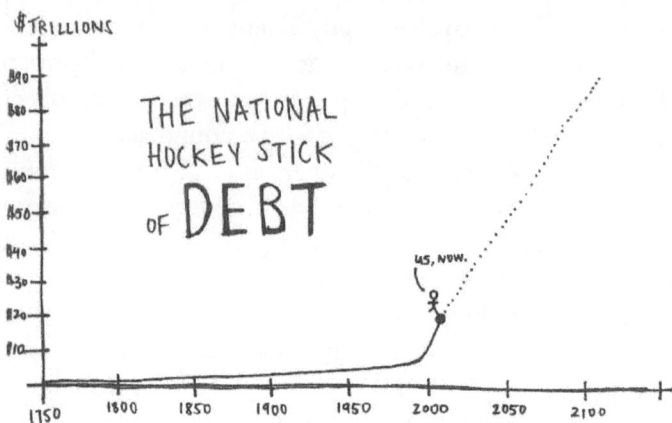

$TRILLIONS

THE NATIONAL
HOCKEY STICK
OF DEBT

US, NOW.

The base of the stick (where the puck makes contact) is a slightly upward arching growth trajectory – solid but unspectacular. Then some great event happens to the business and it just takes off vertically, growing like crazy and constantly doubling (like the handle of the stick). When you're talking about a company's revenue, this is a great thing and you just hope you own some stock. Unfortunately, we're looking at this same growth trajectory when it comes to the amount of money we owe. We have a hockey stick of indebtedness. At least I finally found the good news I was searching for earlier: I figured out why most Americans hate hockey.

If I had to pick a metaphor for the America of the 1900s, it would be *innovative factory to the world*. If I had to pick a metaphor or twenty-first century America, it would be, sadly, *debtor to the world*. While we collect a great deal of money in taxes, it's important to remember that America was founded upon a tax-revolt. The Boston Tea Party being just the first of America's many collective eruptions over taxes. Their amount, the complicated tax filing process, and the Rorschach test about fairness—all make taxes a toxic topic. The reality is that tax revenues affect government services, our national debt, and even unemployment. Yet, for such an important topic, little of the public discussion makes any sense.

Trump's latest tax plan calls for $10 trillion in tax cuts.[59] Considering what we already owe, and what we're projected to, this seems like a curious plan.

While Trump has stated his support for a flat tax, he has stopped short of claiming he'd implement it. Back in the 2012 campaign, Herman Cain skyrocketed to fame on the back of his 9-9-9 flat tax proposal. I mention Cain because I appreciate his robustness. He proposed replacing all taxes with one rate: a 9% tax rate across personal income, business transactions, and federal sales tax. This actually covers the major categories of taxes that I want to talk about— personal taxes, corporate taxes, and consumption taxes.

Personal Taxes

America has used a progressive tax system since 1913. In a progressive system, the tax rate increases along with income level. Using something called *marginal rates*, the increased rate is only paid on the last chunk of income.

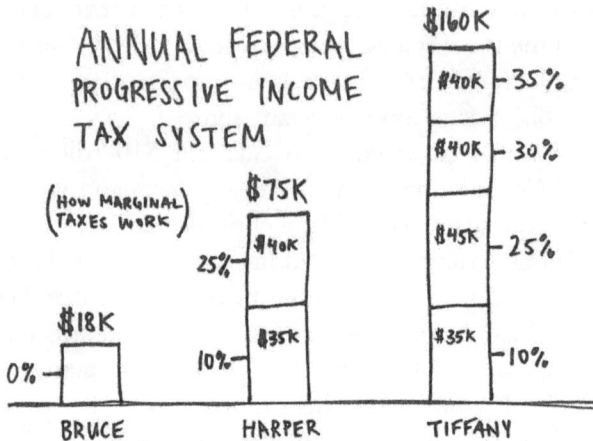

ANNUAL FEDERAL PROGRESSIVE INCOME TAX SYSTEM

(HOW MARGINAL TAXES WORK)

BRUCE — $18K — 0%

HARPER — $75K — $40K 25%, $35K 10%

TIFFANY — $160K — $40K 35%, $40K 30%, $45K 25%, $35K 10%

In the example above, Bruce pays no federal tax because he made so little. Harper earned $75K, and paid 10% on the first $35K and 25% on that last $40K of income. Tiffany made bank, pulling in $160K, and initially paid the same rates as Harper, but then 30% on the amount between $80K and $120K and 35% on the amount between $120K and $160K. Theoretically this system is designed to be both fair and practical.

In terms of fairness, it helps folks cover basic needs. Having Bruce pay no taxes helps him afford some of his basics and ensures that taxes don't discourage him from working (and instead claiming welfare, etc). By gradually increasing the rates, someone like Harper keeps more money for necessities like rent, food, and diapers but still incentivizes people to try to make more. Tiffany makes enough money to afford what some might consider luxuries, so the tax rate she pays on that extra income is also higher.

Practically speaking, given that income and wealth is unevenly distributed, a progressive tax also has the benefit of raising a lot more revenue. 20% of Americans control 85% of the wealth, and so a graduated tax rate ends up being a very big deal.[60]

Proponents of a flat tax system argue that fairness dictates that everyone pay roughly the same relative amount in taxes. However, given the unequal distributions of income, a true flat tax raises way less money than the current system. Since federal spending already far outstrips tax revenue, a pure flat tax without a clear plan for spending cuts should be referred to by the technical tax term of *stupid*. Federal spending far outstrips tax revenue and the US collects a smaller percentage in taxes from its citizens than the rest of the world. In the developed world, the average collected in taxes is 34% of economic product. In the US, that number is just under 25%.[61] So, unless a candidate has plans to massively, *massively* cut spending, ideas like a pure flat tax are fantasy.

"Flat tax" has become something of a marketing term. It can also refer to a dramatically simplified tax code featuring only a handful of basic deductions, a few levels of exempted income, and then a lower overall tax rate. In reality, I'd consider this more of a "progressive flat tax," which is a very legitimate proposal. It's just simplifying the tax code by removing levels and most deductions. Countries like Hong Kong already use such a system and have achieved positive results.

The Bible consists of roughly 775 *thousand* words. The entire tax code is over 9 *million* words long.[62] Anyone who has ever tried to do anything even slightly complicated with their taxes understands why tax preparation is a multi-billion dollar industry and why the IRS employs over 90,000 people.[63] It's a painful system. However, for those who can afford to hire tax specialists, the tax code is like buried treasure with its tax loopholes and special shelters for those who know where to look.

There are effectively two tax systems—the basic one you and I know about and the *other* one. Two decades ago, the 400 highest earners paid roughly 28% of their income in taxes, by 2012 that figure had fallen to 17%.[64] The very wealthiest Americans have a system for dealing with taxes that involve trusts and other complicated tax vehicles to shelter income. All of this almost flips our tax system from progressive to regressive. The very wealthiest decrease their effective income tax rates dramatically thanks to their creative armies of lawyers, accountants, and other specialists.

Corporate Taxes

While that all sounds bad, the business tax issues might be worse. The most repeated knock against the corporate tax system is that American companies have to pay a 35% tax rate, which is the highest in the world. While a good sound-bite, it's meaningless. Due to an obscene litany of tax shelters, breaks, deductions, and other loopholes, American companies pay an average effective rate of 12.6%. Even taking into account all taxes—foreign, national, state, and local—the rate paid would be 16.9%,[65] not even half the stated rate.

A *New York Times* examination of one of America's oldest companies, General Electric, revealed that despite worldwide profits of $14.2 billion (of which only $5.1 billion was in the US), the company paid *zero* in US federal taxes in 2010.[66] It's not just General Electric, either. Consider the (beautiful) MacBook I'm typing this on. Apple, like most multinational companies, employs a small army of tax specialists who help them minimize, or avoid, taxes. In 2011, Apple made $34 billion in profits and paid taxes of $3.3 billion. That comes out to a little less than 10%.[67] That's the amount paid globally—not the amount Apple paid the US government—which was presumably a lot less. We don't know the amount, since Apple declined to break out that amount.

I don't mean to pick on Apple or General Electric, but this tax behavior is the rule, not the exception. My employer for the first five years of my career, Procter & Gamble, is both one of America's most admired companies and also a prolific tax dodger. However, since I'm sort of an Apple fanboy, let's stick to that company. Apple has over $200 billion on their balance sheet. More interesting, over ninety-percent of this cash is held abroad and can't be used in America without being subject to a tax rate that Apple is unwilling to pay.[68] That amount is Apple's overseas profits after they've paid some amount of foreign tax. Apple's position is that they shouldn't be double-taxed. With this money trapped abroad, Apple can't use it to invest in domestic factory expansion, American workers, marketing, or even dividends. Apple, along with nearly every other multi-national company, has called for corporate tax reform so they can bring this money home.

Every other G-8 country, and eighty-percent of industrialized democracies, have some form of a tax system where companies owe taxes only on the income earned domestically.[69] The current American system would instead call for Apple to pay the 35% corporate tax rate on the $191 billion of offshore cash. Not surprisingly, Apple and her shareholders are not crazy about this idea. So, our system ranks as the worst in the world.

All the same, this doesn't sound great on Apple's part either, right? You and I pay taxes on our income, so why shouldn't the richest company in the world also pay into the system? In a perfect world, they would. In reality, we have *inversions*.

In a deal that even Trump called "disgusting," Pfizer merged with the Irish company, Allergen, in 2015's largest "inversion." The inversion converted Pfizer from an American company to an Irish one and dramatically lowered their corporate tax rate to that of their new "home" country's rate. Inversions have become the hottest trend in mergers and acquisitions because the decreased taxes that result *hugely* boost earnings. Over fifty-five such deals have occurred in recent years.[70] While politicians raise a ruckus about this being disgusting or unpatriotic, and even threatening to somehow ban the practice, I think they miss the point or are just posturing.

Inversions feel like the second coming of factories moving overseas. Both inversions and outsourcing were seen as a guaranteed profit-booster, and a benefit to companies of the global economic war. Yet, it further divorces the fate of once-American businesses from that of America and her workers. In light of the never-ending quest for profit-boosters, it's inevitable that the practice will continue until tax policies are reformed.

Inversion is perfectly legal and that's the issue. As an amoral optimization exercise, these companies have done their duty by being loyal to profits and serving shareholders. It's the responsibility of American leaders to design our policies and systems in the interest of long-term economic and employment health. It's a loyalty to American citizens and a duty they have failed to perform.

As a result of the overall Washington gridlock, comprehensive tax reform has barely been addressed. Ironically, it has the makings of perfect bipartisan legislation: cutting taxes (a theoretical favorite of the Right) to allow the repatriation of funds, tied to incentives for "re-shoring" American jobs and domestic investment (a theoretical favorite of the Left). And yet.

Consumption Taxes

Both of the taxes we've talked about—personal income and business profits—are production taxes. A consumption tax is the opposite; it's collected when money is spent. Taxing consumption instead of production incentivizes society to *produce* versus *consume*, resulting in economic reinvestment. The criticism of a consumption tax is that it can be regressive. Citizens who earn the least will typically spend all their money on basic items that are taxed, such as food and transportation, whereas a progressive tax system tries to limit this group's burden from taxes. This is typically resolved by creating an exempted category of "basic goods."

The most common form of a consumption tax and one we are already aware of is a sales tax. In America it's used on the local level and collected when a variety of goods are purchased to help fund state and local governments.

Another form of a consumption tax, as mentioned in the last chapter, is a Value-Added Tax (VAT). While not well known in America, VAT's are pretty much standard across the rest of the world. Similar to the sales tax, it's collected from consumers when they buy something. The difference is that, at every stage of production, an incremental tax is collected from, but ultimately returned to, the business. Without going into too much detail, the important thing to understand is that the cost of a VAT is entirely born by consumers, not businesses. All that added complexity is to leave a traceable "paper" trail that helps prevent tax evasion.

One of the notable characteristics of a VAT is that it generates revenue regardless of where an item was produced. Whether imported from China, or made in Ohio, the item is taxed the same and generates revenue. As previously discussed, this is a *huge* deal for American businesses, since it helps them price more competitively whether they sell to American consumers or export goods. The revenue from a federal VAT could then be used to pay for worker benefits (such as healthcare, unemployment, disability, etc). When the government helps to fund these things instead of relying on businesses, it decreases the cost disadvantage that American workers face against foreign labor.

A consumption-based tax and delinking healthcare from employment (see the healthcare chapter that follows) would be a really scary policy change, but is also a game-changer in the battle to help American blue-collar workers compete globally. So, to summarize, we've ended up with a complicated and punitive tax code that is full of loopholes, costs American jobs, and collects far less revenue than needed. Back to the Jedi-Master of Bankruptcy, Donald Trump. While busy guiding one of his four companies through bankruptcy, it's probably safe to assume he worked on decreasing expenses and increasing revenues to attain positive cash flow. Against this backdrop it's curious that none of his proposed plans does those things.

The 2015 budget calls for spending $3.8 trillion[71] and looks a little like this:

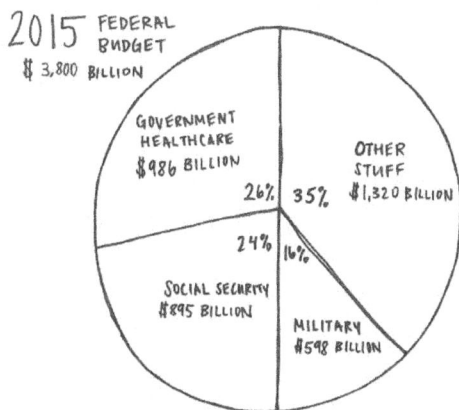

2015 FEDERAL BUDGET
$ 3,800 BILLION

GOVERNMENT HEALTHCARE $986 BILLION — 26%

OTHER STUFF $1,320 BILLION — 35%

SOCIAL SECURITY $895 BILLION — 24%

MILITARY $598 BILLION — 16%

As you can see, healthcare and social security make up nearly half of the government's spending last year. Healthcare spending and social security fall into the category of *Mandatory Spending* since they're part of programs that aren't annually designed, but instead are dictated by eligibility rules. Making changes to mandatory spending basically requires reforming the underlying program—something outside of the budget process. Two-thirds of annual spending is tied up in such mandatory spending.

Military spending *is* part of the yearly discretionary spending set in the budgeting process. While the nearly $600 billion[72] in defense spending is estimated at sixteen-percent of the total federal budget, that's actually its lowest level in twenty years.[73] Conservatively, even if you added up the next seven countries together, we'd still be the number one spender.[74]

On the revenue side, it's hard to fix the tax system, since closing a loophole means taking money out of someone's pocket. As a result, the only provisions that are easy to repeal are the ones that no one is profiting from (which, of course, don't cost anything). When you're dealing with thousands of pages of legislation that hardly anyone even reads, those with influence are able to sneak in highly specific provisions that benefit them. It's easy for these provisions to go unnoticed because they are usually so niche-based and arcane. Yet, for "those in the know," it's quite lucrative. A recent study highlighted an especially egregious, but not unique, case with a company earning a return on investment (ROI) of twenty-two *thousand*-percent on lobbying fees spent on a tax break.[75] Taken together, it's death from a thousand paper cuts. Sadly, this benefit isn't equal opportunity. Here's a quote in *BusinessWeek* from the president of a small Ohio manufacturing company:

> *"We can't afford to buy the (tax) preferences and it's tough for us to keep track of them. Big business is getting the better end of this because they have money to spend."*[76]

Since taxes are so easy to demonize, there's very little political upside to fixing our tax system. That's how we end up with Trump proposing $10 trillion in tax cuts. If he, or anyone else, actually tried to fix the system, those who'd lose special tax benefits would fight tooth and nail to prevent it, while the rest of us would find the whole topic so complicated that we wouldn't really want to talk about it. The result: the politician who tries to improve the tax system instead of campaigning on gimmicks— proposing, for example, something that will bring in sufficient revenue and be fairer and simpler for everyone—will be attacked mercilessly while having few defenders. Politicians are dumb, but they're not that dumb.

On the corporate side, we must accept that we live in a ruthlessly competitive global marketplace and that companies no longer feel a responsibility to their native country. Other nations, hungrily looking to add new jobs, will use massive incentives to attract that next factory or corporate headquarters to their shores. That's why America needs a globally competitive tax system. The new corporate tax rate should be significantly lower than the current thirty-five-percent, without the current loopholes, while rewarding investment in American jobs with tax credits. This means replacing today's high sticker price system, its incredible complexity, and penalties on investment in America, with the opposite—simplicity and incentives. This dovetails with adopting the consumption based tax system to help pay for what are currently employer provided benefits. It's a scary wholesale change, but when you're starting with a disastrous tax code, you have little choice.

On the individual taxpayer side, reform to raise sufficient revenue and simplify the code involves eliminating deductions. Considering the popularity of many of those deductions, such as the interest deduction on a home's mortgage, this'll be a complicated and messy debate. The hope is that we'd be willing to make these tradeoffs as part of a comprehensive plan that simplifies the system, makes it more equitable, and shores up confidence in America's long-term fiscal health.

Then again, maybe that's the genius of the whole Trump argument, after all. By 2024, having successfully passed a $10 trillion dollar cut and not decreasing spending, America will have passed the point of no return, necessitating the Trump specialty: *Bankruptcy*.

Considering how he managed to emerge from his litanies of corporate bankruptcies personally unscathed—perhaps counting on him to perform this same magic for America isn't the worst idea. He'd be able to then write *The Art of the Bankruptcy* and it would be a bestseller for the ages, giving The Donald quite the legacy and maybe even a place among the all-time Presidential greats.

As Americans, we have to answer the question of what exactly it's worth to leave a solvent nation to our kids. The nice thing about budgets is that they're simple math, not rocket science. Since we actually did once send someone to the moon in a rocket ship (and now billionaires like Elon Musk and Jeff Bezos are doing it!), I'm pretty sure, if we really wanted to, we could handle this, too.

BONUS HIDDEN CHAPTER!
HEALTHCARE:
A SICK SYSTEM

"I'm a conservative on most issues but a liberal on health. It is an unacceptable but accurate fact that the number of uninsured Americans has risen to 42 million. Working out detailed plans will take time. But the goal should be clear: Our people are our greatest asset. We must take care of our own. We must have universal healthcare.

Our objective [should be] to make reforms for the moment and, longer term, to find an equivalent of the single-payer plan that is affordable, well administered, and provides freedom of choice. Possible? The good news is, yes. There is already a system in place—the Federal Employees Health Benefits Program—that can act as a guide for all healthcare reform. It operates through a centralized agency that offers considerable range of choice. While this is a government program, it is also very much market-based. It allows six-hundred twenty private insurance companies to compete for this market. Once a year participants can choose from plans which vary in benefits and costs".[77]

– Donald Trump

Fifteen years ago, Trump looked admiringly to Canada and spoke in favor of a national, government-led, single payer system. In a post-Obamacare world, this kind of talk is heresy. Today he shuns any such language to instead call for an amorphous plan of private competition. Give that Obamacare ruled out single-payer in favor of a private market exchanges, this doesn't sound materially different, but Trump doesn't agree. He's called Obamacare a "catastrophe that needs to be repealed and replaced." While still supporting the notion of universal coverage, he hasn't shared any detail beyond wanting to increase competition.

I'm almost sympathetic to Trump here. He's had to tie himself into pretzels because the system is such a mess and the Republican base has been trained to see the law as evil. Given its massive role in the economy, its potential to bankrupt America, and as one of the most polarizing issues in politics, I want to share the important context of healthcare.

I spent many hundreds of hours during my Congressional campaign in 2010 reading about the healthcare market and speaking with some staffers who helped write the bill to understand its intent. With all of that behind me, I've done my best to simplify. Like a patient who hasn't gone to the doctor in years, only finally to show up in really bad shape, our system is in trouble. It's all painfully complicated, but I want to make three main points:

1) How enormous healthcare spending is
2) Cliff Notes on the worst parts
3) How the system contributes to unemployment

1) We Spend 17% of GDP (and Climbing) on Healthcare

Healthcare spending is make-your-head-explode massive. From hospitals, individual doctors' offices, pharmaceutical companies, insurers, and everything else in between, we're spending close to $3.0 trillion.[78] At 17% of our GDP, that's basically seventeen dollars spent on healthcare from every one-hundred dollars America produces. $3.0 trillion is a lot of money, but we're also a big country. To figure out how to think about spending

17% of our wealth on healthcare, let's do what I did back in school and cheat...err, peek at our neighbors' answers. Germany spends eleven-percent, Canada ten-percent, Sweden nine-percent, the UK and Japan eight-percent.[79] We spend seventeen-percent.

Unfortunately, despite spending the most in the world (both in-total and per person), we're also not really getting the best care overall. We get the best care for some things, but in other areas, it's not even close. Compared to other rich countries, we do worse for chronic conditions like diabetes and asthma because we have higher rates of complications and hospitalizations, but do better on treating critical illnesses, with among the highest survival rates for cancers and strokes.[80] We are better on the edges at treating the most severe issues, but don't do as well in the vast middle. It stands to reason that if we could do better with preventative care and in treating chronic conditions, we might be able to nip many expensive health issues in the bud.

Overall, the average American's life expectancy is slightly below the world average, though that's hard to pin on just the healthcare system. So many of us smoke, fail to exercise, eat (delicious) fast food (which causes obesity) and other not-so-good things that factor in. This much is certain: we're spending a lot more than everyone else, but we're not getting a lot more for all that money. If I were an especially surly Surya, I'd say that we're getting less than those who pay less. "Pay more, get less" isn't the best slogan to spend trillions of dollars on.

Back to that $3 trillion in annual spending: Our government is responsible for the biggest chunk. Through Medicare and Medicaid, the government's share is roughly one-third of total healthcare dollars.[81] Counting the Veterans Administration and other programs, it comes to about half of the total amount.[82] With lots of Baby Boomers set to retire, that bill's going to climb much, much higher. In 2012 when I last wrote on America's issues, health care costs were fifteen-percent of GDP; now, in 2016, it's up to seventeen-percent and projected to reach around twenty-percent in the next few years.[83]

2) A Highlight Reel of Healthcare Dysfunction

We pay the bulk of the world's prescription R&D bill

Almost every other country negotiates to set the price drug companies can charge their citizens *before* granting them access to sell the drug. America allows these companies to charge us whatever they wish, so it's not shocking that we pay the most in the world for nearly every prescription drug. This allows clowns like pseudo-Wu Tang Clan fan Martin Shkreli to buy a pharmaceutical company and then raise the price of a life-saving drug by five-*thousand* percent.[84] There are other companies that do similar things, with Valeant being the biggest and most famous example.

On average, we pay *twice* as much for drugs as citizens of other industrialized nations.[85] While everyone gets the same drugs, America foots the bill for the world. Sort of like how neoconservatives want us to be the world's policeman, our healthcare system makes us the world's pharmacist. We subsidize the world's drug bills.

Insurance used to be only for healthy people

Since we have an employer-based healthcare system, I lost my coverage in 2009 when I quit my job to run for

Congress. Despite being young, handsome, and healthy, I wanted to buy insurance to be a responsible adult, but, *surprise*! They wouldn't let me. Four years earlier, I had weird joint pain and consulted with a bunch of doctors. Ultimately, they had no clue, told me to rub some dirt on it, and not to worry. Now, years later, the insurance companies, concerned about those visits to specialists, ignored the fact that I was never diagnosed with anything, and denied me coverage on the basis of a pre-existing condition (I'd assume arthritis). Reassuringly, they did tell me a number of times that they were really sorry.

Eventually I got a manager on the phone, explained that I was running for Congress (key phrase), that I didn't have arthritis, that I thought they were jerks, and that I kind of couldn't wait to talk to the media about their shady practices. Since this was at a time when the insurers were battling the White House over health care reform, I shouldn't have been shocked when I got a call back a few hours later telling me that I was approved. This wasn't a huge deal since I was actually healthy, but what if I had been sick with some debilitating, pre-existing condition?

I bring this up to point out how screwed up the insurance industry is. Historically, this was how insurers competed for profits. The factors that determined industry profits failed to improve quality of care or decrease overall prices.

One of the main factors that *did* determine profits was selecting the healthiest patients. As I just shared, in the vein of "better safe than sorry," this included not insuring anyone who they thought might be sick (like 2009 Surya!). That makes twisted sense because the insurance company that only insured young, healthy people would keep all those premium dollars and not need to pay out much in reimbursements for treatments.

This seemed really bad until I read more about their second favorite tool to drive profits: rescission. That's where you have insurance, but once you start racking up medical bills for an ailment, your insurance company does a deep-dive investigation into your records to find a reason to terminate your coverage. If they find any evidence you might have had a pre-existing condition, they'd use it to try to drop you. If somewhere along the way you had missed a payment, then your coverage might be considered lapsed and, "sorry, no insurance policy for you since, oh look, it appears you have a pre-existing condition."

Obamacare now outlaws these practices, but just a few years ago, insurance companies made their profits by figuring out ways not to pay the medical bills of sick people. It's going to take quite a while for insurance companies to get used to competing in the new system.

A baffling system designed to raise—not lower—prices

I went out to (an imaginary) dinner last night and they gave me a menu without prices. I ordered a hamburger and at the end of my meal got a bill for $250. After I freaked out and asked why, I was told that the kitchen had a lot of trouble getting the beef, the lettuce was more expensive than usual, they brought on some experts to oversee the cooking process, and since I sat at the bar, that was going to cost extra, too. They showed me the itemized list of all this crap, with a price next to each, and it added up to $250.

That's pretty much how all healthcare works, because *doctors and hospitals get paid for actions, not results.* Some ninety-nine-percent of healthcare dollars are paid individually for each visit, x-ray, procedure, or medicine—not for the successful outcome that resolves why you needed treatment in the first place. In other words, I just wanted a hamburger, but got the drama of how it was made, instead.

At worst, medical providers do what we've financially incentivized them to do, generate as much income as possible by ordering extra tests, extra procedures, and scheduling more visits than necessary. Whereas, in the real world, I'd be willing to pay more for a better burger—*if* it tasted better, was healthier for me and delivered faster, etc.—but it would have to *be* better. Instead, in Bizarro Healthcare Land, the way someone gets paid more for the burger would be by making preparing it as *complicated as possible* before serving it.

While it's bad enough that those extra procedures make the system more expensive, they also carry the risk of complications. Hospital stays and surgical procedures "just to be safe" increase the risk of infection or medical error. Fee-for-service doesn't just generate unneeded extra costs, but also extra treatments that can actually *lead* to worst medical outcomes. The Institute of Medicine has estimated we waste $750 *billion* annually in unnecessary treatments, inefficient delivery, excess administrative costs, inflated prices, fraud, and preventable failures.[86]

Even the healthcare providers not influenced in any way by money can feel pressured to order extra procedures due to the prevalence of malpractice suits. Doctors are encouraged to "go through the motions" and pile on tests, this way if a patient later sues, their thoroughness can be used as a defense.

In the real world, prices for everything from TVs to cell phones consistently march lower. Over time, we have always gotten better products for less money. Companies compete by trying to have the best product (and making sure we *know* it's better) and/or by offering it at the lowest cost. To survive and grow, the most successful companies constantly improve both cost and quality. This isn't magic or an accident – it's the natural result of a properly functioning market where companies compete for consumer dollars. But. Not. Healthcare.

As "consumers" of healthcare, we're trained *not* to care how much things cost. We pay our twenty-dollar co-pay and the rest is someone else's problem. The cost of the tests, medicine, or any of the rest is irrelevant, because we're spending someone else's money. This separation between the person who *pays* and the person who *selects* prevents the market from doing its normal *better/cheaper* magic. Going back to that imaginary hamburger dinner— would I have even cared how much it cost if I just paid a dollar-ninety-five co-pay and left with a full stomach?

Not to beat a dead cow, but one last hamburger reference. Last night, I couldn't even use Yelp to decide where to get my imaginary burger-as-a-metaphor-for-healthcare dinner. In addition to menus without prices, I also had to deal with choosing a restaurant without having any reviews or other information. It's a bit sad that we have so much more information on the restaurant down the street than about our healthcare. Lacking this basic transparency, we end up choosing based on random information like which doctor or hospital is closest. Unable to reward the best providers with more business, and punish the worst providers by avoiding them, we fail to incentivize the behavior (aka *better* care at a *better* price) we're looking for.

I'll now drop the Big O—Obamacare (a. k. a. the Affordable Care Act)—and point out that, as part of it, some of these things are now relics of the past. Pre-existing conditions and rescission in particular, are now illegal, but it's important to remember that, until now, since this was how the money in healthcare was made, the system will need to evolve and it'll be slow. The new system is theoretically designed to make the new factors that drive profitability how *effective* and *efficient* patient care is, and *not* the old factors, like competing to only insure healthy people or how many extra treatments could be ordered. That's what the hope is, anyway.

3) Healthcare System = Major Cause of Unemployment

One of the most important, but least understood, things about our healthcare system is that it's directly related to our national unemployment struggles. To explain, we need to return to that idealized-America, circa WWII.

As the US fought in Europe and Asia during World War II, inflation was the major economic concern back home. American factories worked around-the-clock to produce planes and weapons for the war effort. This pushed the prices of everything from worker wages to everyday goods higher, since there wasn't enough to meet the demand. Price instability causes so many problems for an economy, so the government tried to fight inflation by freezing prices and workers' wages.

With wages frozen, companies could no longer compete to attract new workers by offering more money. Instead they got creative in how they enticed new employees to join the workforce by offering other benefits, namely health insurance. Workers and companies paid taxes on wages, but benefits like health insurance were exempted and treated as a business expense. This had far reaching effects *after* WWII, because this system of not taxing health insurance benefits remained. Thanks to the tax benefit, it was cheaper for employers to buy health insurance for employees, so it developed as essentially an accident of history how Americans came about getting their healthcare from employers.

Providing healthcare to employees is a significant expense for both small-businesses and global companies. Every other rich nation has some form of national healthcare. In these systems, healthcare is not paid by employers, but from the pool of taxes. In labor-intensive industries like automobile manufacturing, this difference in who pays for workers' benefits has significant consequences. It's one of the main reasons why Detroit automakers have located so much production just over the Michigan border in neighboring Canadian cities, in Mexico, and throughout the world (as mentioned in the *Hecho en China* section).

In the past 10 years, insurance premiums have gone up by one-hundred-thirteen-percent.[87] With healthcare costs rapidly rising, uncertainty about future costs has given management another reason to be skittish about hiring domestically. Looking ahead, there are many reasons to be optimistic about improving healthcare and its economics. Let's look at three simple ideas and trends that I'm particularly excited about.

1) Leveraging Technology:

While technology has helped transform many other industries, medical infrastructure has lagged. One of the largest causes of unnecessary tests and missed diagnoses is a lack of basic patient information. That's where Electronic Medical Records (EMRs) come in. Having an electronic history of past tests, symptoms, ailments, and medicines would allow faster, more effective treatment.

All of this patient data serves as the foundation for evidence-based medicine. As the results of different courses of treatments for a condition are automatically logged and analyzed, healthcare professionals will know what types of treatments get the best results for different situations—how Netflix's algorithm learns which movies to recommend, but to save lives and trillions of dollars. EMRs, in conjunction with a health information exchange, allow data to be available to all medical providers when it's needed most. This can lead to improved quality of care and lower costs through decreased duplicate tests, allergic reactions, and the like. While it'll cause a lot of short-term pain for the system, more aggressively pushing the digitization of medicine lays the foundation for saving money and improving results in the long run.

2) Operationalizing Medicine:

In a 2012, a *New Yorker* article by Atul Gawande discussed how The Cheesecake Factory[88] offered a great, if weird roadmap for our healthcare system. There are hundreds of outposts for the restaurant chain around the country that consistently offer cheap, tasty food despite a huge menu that's dozens of pages long. In the private sector, the kind of operational excellence to pull this off is pretty standard practice. Companies look at an employee that does something well, breaks down how they're able to do it (step-by-step), and then figures out how to teach this successfully to everyone else. Surprisingly, this isn't common in medicine. Bringing the scientific method to medicine through "evidence-based medicine" would allow us to standardize what works and save the costs of unnecessary treatment while delivering better health outcomes.

3) <u>Incentivizing Outcomes:</u>

If we compensated healthcare providers for successful treatment instead of each test ordered, we would motivate America's medical community to heal in the most effective, cost-efficient way possible. This is similar to how the private sector looks to standardize best practices to get "better and cheaper." As discussed earlier, the current "fee-for-service" system drives the exact opposite result.

∞β∞

More than five years after its inception, Obamacare remains the dirty word of politics. Democrats and Republicans both wish it would just go away. However, due to the effectiveness of the demonization campaign (Death Panelssssss!!!) during the debate over the bill, it's heresy for a Republican to do anything but slam it. The reality is that it can't and *won't* be repealed. To take away coverage away from tens of millions or go back to the days of denying coverage based on pre-existing conditions and rescission would be political suicide. Yet, this same legislation is an incredibly complicated instrument that needs to be fine-tuned and sharpened. So while the law might be safe from repeal, in order to be effective, it's absolutely critical that it be updated and adjusted to drive down costs or we're all screwed. There are many reasons for optimism, but if the healthcare conversation remains toxic, we risk allowing the largest expense in our budget to spiral out of control. With all of

Trump's calls to stop China from kicking our economic derrieres and to cut the national debt—healthcare is unquestionably the key to both. It's where any rational businessman would start.

REALITY TV ELECTIONS

"The average American doesn't want to be educated; he doesn't want to improve his mind; he doesn't even want to work, consciously, at being a good citizen .... [T]here are two ways you can interest him in a campaign and only two that we have ever found successful. You can put on a fight (he likes a good hot battle, with no punches pulled), or you can put on a show (he likes the movies; he likes mysteries; he likes fireworks and parades): So if you can't fight, PUT ON A SHOW! And if you put on a good show, Mr. and Mrs. America will turn out to see it." [89]

Are elections the original Reality TV show? Probably. The above quote isn't about Trump. It's from America's very first political consultants, Whitaker and Baxter, back in 1934. It's strange that something as important as the process of selecting our national leaders—the people who launch wars, make critical financial decisions, and set the policies that govern so much of our lives—is done in such a vapid way.

Given Trump's role as the world's biggest reality TV star, it's easy to think this started with him, but as I was researching this book, I remembered reading about the first of the 1960 Presidential debates between JFK and Nixon. Kennedy looked tan and, thanks to some well-applied makeup, well-rested—projected quite the commanding presence. By contrast, Nixon's pale skin, dark bags under his eyes, and copious sweating painted a picture of a man with something to hide. Those listening to the debate on the radio picked Nixon as the winner; those watching the events on TV preferred Kennedy. While it's debatable whether the survey of radio listeners skewed Republican and those predisposed to Nixon,[90] the essence remained—image mattered. Fortunately for Kennedy, that was the first ever broadly televised debate and a large part of the "Camelot" mystique to come could be traced back to how well the Kennedys captivated America's attention through the media. Even then, there were many who decried the superficiality behind how the electorate was influenced.

While he may not have JFK's youth and vitality, with his experiences across more than ten seasons of *The Apprentice*, Trump clearly has the edge on his rivals. It comes across clearly on the campaign trail.

One of the first things that jumped out at me about Trump's campaign was his mastery of sound bites. Just as he popularized *You're Fired*, Trump has simplified the issues roiling the electorate into infectious sound bites: *Walls around Mexico*, *Cutting the head off ISIS*, *Banning Muslims*, or, *Make America Great Again*. It's also why I think Trump is so great at Twitter: 140 characters is basically a sound bite. On *The Apprentice*, Trump knew he had to land the line and move on due to the nature of the editing on the show. Whether in the vaunted boardroom or on a task, Trump would always use clear, memorable language to make his points. Even when what's coming out of his mouth annoys me, I find myself strangely captivated by what he might say next.

I had to watch my season of *The Apprentice really* to learn about editing. While the producers never used editing to outright lie, I was portrayed as a super Type A, who lacked a sense of humor, and any people skills. While that's not exactly how I am, I can be pretty intense and, because I didn't trust the producers, I basically stripped myself of quirks to do my best robot impression. Since more than a few people in my life have described me as a six-year-old, I recognize "Apprentice Surya" for what he was: a convenient caricature of what the camera captured.

Trump has brought this knowledge into the election cycle in a big way. Similar to the role of producers and editors on a reality TV show, the media makes caricatures of candidates. Nuance is tough in politics, so it's the gaffes and broad strokes that fit the media's convenient narratives. No one understands this better than Donald Trump.

One of the real genius moves of Trump's campaign not broadly understood is how he's effectively made a caricature of himself *before* the media could. This drives his critics crazy and leads to them looking down on him. He can come across as a simplistic cartoon character, yet, I'm arguing it's actually strategy, a *feature*, not a *bug*. Trump is speaking directly to his core base of supporters and they love what others see as excessive. His brash, simplistic, divisive language is what has powered his campaign. He's made a caricature out of himself on *his* terms. *The Apprentice* might have aired on NBC, but Trump has proven crazy like a Fox.

I almost feel bad for the other candidates. Trump has a decade of experience starring in and producing a reality TV show that's gotten him into peak fighting weight. It's one of the reasons he hasn't had to use that big advantage he keeps reminding us of—his immense wealth to self-fund his campaign. While Trump talks up the fact that self-funding means he can't be bought like his opponents, he hasn't yet had to spend real money because the 2016 election cycle has basically been The Donald Trump Show. In 2015, the evening newscasts featured nearly four hours of coverage about him between January and November, whereas Ted Cruz, the current number two in the primaries, got seven *minutes* of coverage.[91] I'll be honest. Until now, I didn't think it was possible to feel sorry for Ted Cruz.

The producers of *The Apprentice* certainly tried to drum up fights. Using the slightest bit of pretense, they'd try to get me to attack another contestant on camera. It's a competition after all, so I suppose they didn't usually have to work very hard to get the contestants attacking each other. This relentless focus on conflict, highlighted so well in the opening quote of this chapter, is also the bread and butter of the media's political coverage. *When Candidates Attack* is always the lead story. Trump's troll game is quite strong and he's managed to mock, bait, and irritate the entire field of GOP candidates—garnering gobs of media attention along the way. Conflict plays well for ratings, both on Reality TV and in politics.

On a darker theme, both reality TV and politics often follow a scorched earth playbook. In military terms, the practice of destroying the resources when leaving an area if they could be useful to an enemy reflects a win-at-all-costs mentality that focuses only on the present, while ignoring long-term consequences.

As I prepared to go on the show, I watched episodes of different reality TV shows and my takeaway was that the producers and editors couldn't be trusted. Because they had taken such liberties (obvious on closer scrutiny) to make their episodes tell the story they wanted, I felt deeply cynical about their intentions and concluded that I'd be an idiot to trust them. Of all the contestants on my season, I had the most adversarial relationship with the producers because I was constantly on guard and distrustful. Of course, I would learn that it wouldn't matter: The process of filming generates so many hours of footage and, with the other contestants reliably narrating whatever story the producers wanted, they end up making exactly the episode they wanted. Still, the degree of manipulation I saw watching the shows, scorched my willingness to trust the producers while I was filming.

In politics, the candidates pander, attack, and lie to get what they want in the short term at the cost of negative, long-term consequences. They may win that election, but voters end up hating all the candidates and grow incredibly cynical about everything in the process. As I look at this 2016 election cycle, I can't help but think the surprising elevation of Bernie Sanders on the Left, and Trump on the Right, is the normal reaction of a populace sick of being fed the same old garbage. The campaigns of yesteryear thoroughly scorched the earth and today, things that look different are in vogue. Politics and elections have felt like a dark joke for a long time now as election after election became flooded with billions in special interest money. The billionaire elites' handpicked candidates dominating primaries, coupled to politicians intentionally complicating already confusing issues, put Trump in position as the *antidote* to all these things.

That's how we've come to this place where we seem to be evaluating something of such importance in seemingly trivial ways. With a substantial part of the electorate feeling insecure by issues that are not easily understood *and* so disgusted by politics in general, is it any wonder that the criteria by which we're hiring our presidents seem not that different from the rules of *The Apprentice?*

The biggest difference between *being* on *The Apprentice* and *watching* it, was how simplified everything became. The plot points became gross over-simplifications (caricatures, remember?), because that's what the audience required. Shades of grey are not as entertaining as Steven being a moron, Suzy being a ditz, Sam being racist, and Surya having no people skills. Viewers tuned in for entertainment and this they were given.

While the last two chapters provided information on relevant economic, security, and fiscal issues, that is only a component of the political scene. Add in politicians who muddy the waters using disingenuous arguments to complicate already complex issues, and it's easy to see the allure of using simpler factors in deciding who to vote for: charisma and "gut" feel.

Also driving elections towards nuclear levels of reality TV is the level of disgust with politics. Certainly, we're not lacking for examples of the absurd or terrible. Lists of the reasons why Americans are cynical about politics justify a dedicated book, but a few are worth a quick mention.

On a local, state, and federal level hardly a month passes without news of a politician directly abusing his position of power to enrich himself, a member of his family, or his business. Close to home, my local representative to the New York Assembly, Sheldon Silver, was just found guilty of multiple counts of corruption involving millions of dollars. He's just one of many who are stealing from the people.

Some of this corruption has even been legalized: Over $3 billion is annually spent lobbying Washington.[92]

This is separate from the billions in campaign contributions raised. We already talked about how screwed up the defense or healthcare industries are, so it's not surprising that those same industries are among the highest lobbying spenders.[93] While it's hard to have a detailed sense of how insidious the impact of money and lobbyists are to the legislative process, I think we all feel it in our gut that the most powerful among us are always working behind-the-scenes to come out ahead.

Even murkier is the "revolving door" between government employees and the very industries they regulate. It might start with a politician receiving donations from the agricultural industry today, and end with a job in the agricultural industry's lobbying firm tomorrow. These politicians might receive multi-million dollar contracts to do nothing other than make introductions to widen a firm's access to the hallowed halls of Washington. Worker bees in lobbying firms might work as staffers in Congress before returning to lobbying with a fatter Rolodex and an increased salary. If I knew that everyone who once had my low-paying job eventually got a huge pay increase by not angering certain groups, wouldn't I think twice (or 100 times) about angering them? This "shadow corruption" is insidious and also hard to identify.

In its worst form this turns into "regulatory capture." This is when the special interest group that is supposed to be regulated by an agency, ends up controlling that agency, akin to when the inmates take over the asylum. A specific regulation that might only have a small impact on the daily lives of all Americans might be critical to a business or industry. While we're barely paying attention—let alone actively campaigning for the policies that protect our collective interests—those being regulated work tirelessly to get what will benefit them. This broadly reflects how money has come to influence politics: Organized greed defeats disorganized democracy.

"Do as I say and not as I do," seems to be the Golden Rule of politics. From delivering lectures on morality while carrying on affairs with staffers, demonizing "deviant lifestyles" while being in the closet, or preaching about fiscal responsibility while spending money like a drunk – the hypocrisy of the never-ending stream of scandals is staggering.

Given the contempt for politics and the complexity of the underlying issues, I see it as natural that elections have devolved into a higher-stakes version of *The Apprentice*. While it seems absurd that this is how we're choosing a president, I remember that ostensibly, *The Apprentice* was a job interview as well as entertainment. While it's strange to watch debates where the candidates are baited into attacking each other and never get into policy specifics, I remember that *The Apprentice's* "business tasks" had me performing a halftime show at a soccer game (the task that got me fired!), selling honey in a grocery store, working a carwash, and modeling a swimsuit for the designer Trina Turk. What would these things have to do with working for a real estate billionaire?

As I watch Trump go nuts on Twitter, savage Ted Cruz, or feature inane song and dance routines at his campaign rallies, I sometimes slip and grow exasperated that this is the interview process to become America's President. At those times, the details of "my televised job interview" come to mind and it all makes sense again. While the other candidates get frustrated with the process or fail to play the right cards, Trump is out there crushing Cruz, Rubio, Bush, Christie, et al. They're sitting at the card table playing blackjack and hoping for a good hand, while Trump, with his PhD in reality TV, is counting the cards.

CONCLUSION

That's the *Donald Trump* I know and some context about the *America* I know. It's a mouthful to explain each time I'm asked for an opinion on Trump and it's my hope that this book will travel more broadly than just my circles. I submit this just days after Trump's convincing Super Tuesday primary wins increased his likelihood of securing the nomination. I continue to believe that Trump's stunning rise is a result of the failure of his detractors to understand his *appeal* and the failure of his supporters to understand *the man*.

Trump has played perfectly to America's current insecurities in ways that go to his strengths of personality. While it's his foreign policy statements that have generated the most headlines, I believe those to be red herrings. They are his most incendiary sound bites because those issues are the easiest to demonize and play best to fear, but it's the economic factors that have driven his rise.

Voter research seems to support my case. Four out of five Trump supporters believe that *all* immigration hurts America more than it helps. More than half say that free trade has been bad for America.[94] He's dominating support among the Republicans concerned about maintaining their standard of living. Likewise, he dominates his opponents among the Republicans who strongly believe that immigrants have weakened American society.[95]

Even as it's invisible to those of us living in big cities and on the coasts, everyday life for thousands of American communities has changed dramatically. While a variety of Band-Aids—credit cards, housing bubbles, and the like—have masked some of the negative impact on households for some time, the trend is clear. As blue-collar, middle class jobs have left America, they've been replaced by jobs at the retail, hospitality, and customer service end of the spectrum. A weakened middle class has driven income inequality to ranges not seen since the Great Depression and created despondency among the millions facing diminished economic prospects.

These changes are also somewhat responsible for revising decades-old narratives. The "drug epidemic" was once code for talking about inner cities and "ghettos." Yet, as factories closed, and the plight of unemployment hung over rural towns all over America, drug problems crept in. Addiction to opiates like heroin and meth has infected America's rural communities. In New Hampshire, twenty-five-percent of those interviewed cited drug abuse as the most pressing concern facing the state, surpassing even employment issues.[96] In some ways, this is the perverse-but-orderly transition of things. In the years after the Civil War, jobs fled the North for the South, leaving ghettos in their wake. This, sadly, played out again in rural America, as jobs fled to China.

When factories close, and drugs infiltrate a community, who's to blame and how do things get better? Trump's potent message is to blame Mexicans for bringing drugs and crime, the Chinese for stealing jobs, and to ban Muslims to protect America. In a complicated world that lacks easy answers, it's a pleasant fiction to believe these so-called *solutions* will fix everything.

A key essence of Trump's gift as a Reality TV figure was his clarity. "The company sponsoring this task is the greatest in the world; That person I'm about to fire is a total failure as a leader; This other TV personality is an absolute dummy." This talent has translated perfectly to politics. Trump's superpower of framing issues superficially and trusting his gut instinct, has allowed him to deliver the message that so many people have been craving, all in his trademark ultra-clear, entertaining, and forceful fashion.

I'm not among those who see Trump's campaign positions as disingenuous. I just think he doesn't look deeply at the issues he talks about, a stance helped by his high opinion of himself. If he eventually figures out the illogic of a position, he just moves on, leaving it in his wake as yesterday's news. From time to time, we all have great ideas that don't survive the test of time. Once we get the obvious part of what we missed, we realize those who were skeptical were right all along. Trump just skips this part and moves on to the next issue. He doesn't seem to suffer from cognitive dissonance because he probably believes that he's the first one to have caught the complication. Unlike most of us, critics and haters get no mindshare in Trump's brain: a key Trump strength *and* weakness.

Another Trump superpower is his narcissism. I don't even need to call up memories of my time with him to assert that he loves attention and adulation. Anyone not living under a rock has seen it on display over the past forty years. When his narcissism meets his superficial thinking, they breed the simplistic solutions that have found voice in his incredible "policy" sound bites ("Build a wall! Take their oil! Register the Muslims!"). His boundless appetite for adulation causes him to keep pushing the envelope with his statements, because he can sense that his audience is yearning for it. They're hurting and, like a religious genius, he wants to lay his hands on the masses to cure them of their employment, debt, and security ailments. Like a cancer patient who has exhausted all medical options—this is what our environment has birthed for so many.

As I campaigned for Congress, I'd often hear that everything went South starting with the ratification of NAFTA (North American Free Trade Agreement) in 1993 and China's 2002 entry to the WTO (World Trade Organization). These dual events triggered the free-for-all of jobs leaving for Mexico and China and things have been changing (not in a good way), since. In both events, the "elites" —the economists and the politicians—all agreed that *everyone* would win. Americans would get cheaper goods and displaced workers would retrain and "move up the value chain." *Everything is awesome!* [97] We certainly got the cheaper goods: a study put the savings per American at between $32 and $61 a year. Across the three-hundred-plus million Americans this means *billions* in annual savings. This is a small benefit for everyone, but devastating for those directly impacted.[98] Yet, manufacturing was never really replaced and the towns and communities that depended on it were altered forever.

Enter a billionaire, who everyone, even in the smallest town in America has heard about, famous for being rich, powerful, and a master strategist. He's told us tales of how he abused the system by bribing politicians to get better treatment, but that he's now going to use all the talent that made him the *most successful* businessman in America to "Make America Great Again."

Franklin Roosevelt came from extreme wealth, but passed sweeping legislation to help lift up the poorest among us and was dubbed a "traitor to his class" for it.[99] From a marketing standpoint, Trump as a similar "traitor to his class," acting on behalf of the working class, has a nice hook to it.

Trump's positioned himself as a sort of War Time President, like Roosevelt, who's not here to make friends or be politically correct. Each time he's attacked by the media and politicians, it reinforces his power in the eyes of his supporters. Trump being attacked by the elites—the same ones who reassured them that the factories could leave and everything would still be okay—is actually proof of his power. Trump's unspoken message is that Trump needs *us* (the voters) to save America from *them* (the elites).

While Trump's campaign slogan of "Make America Great Again" is decidedly optimistic, the notes he hits in speeches focus on the past. It's a veritable Greatest Hits of America's mistakes and failures: The ways in which China has beaten us to take the jobs, how Mexico purportedly sends criminals and undesirables to outnumber us, and that we've screwed up our battle against radical Islam requiring extreme measures like banning them from America. There are no specifics behind the how of these things, there's just the laying on of the hands. Hallelujah!

This is unfortunate because, despite the severity of our budget, national security, and electoral process challenges, there are many reasons for optimism. In some ways this also highlights another aspect of our Reality TV politics. As I listened to Obama's 2016 State of the Union address, I found it remarkable for its positive view of America and her future. Conversely, I find listening to Trump and other Republican presidential candidates remarkable for the negativity on the state of things. There's little nuance and we've essentially been forced to listen to caricatured versions of reality. The truth, as it usually is, is somewhere in between. I believe that many of each side's concerns are very real, but so are our advantages and opportunities to resolve them for the better.

In the future, I expect automation to start working in our favor. The use of intelligent robots has already significantly accelerated in industry and even medicine, leading many experts to predict that robots will replace a significant amount of human labor in the coming years.[100] While this will decrease the amount of manufacturing jobs, it also means that labor will become a significantly smaller piece of overall manufacturing costs.

In addition, the combination of rising foreign labor costs, shipping costs, and a desire for better intellectual property protection will increase the number of companies looking to bring back the production of goods sold in America. This is already happening, but there's actually a shortage of workers with the proper training and skills.[101] Common sense programs like retooling our community college system to help support this kind of training will make a huge difference.

I'm even more confident we can fix our healthcare problems. Thanks to the best medical schools in the world (and through immigration), we're already blessed with the most talented supply of physicians. Combined with our historical strength in entrepreneurial spirit, we can set the world standard for cost-efficient, high-quality healthcare. Healthcare is basically a solved problem for much of the world, so the answers are everywhere around us. Leveraging technology, changing incentives, and standardizing best practices offer the potential to dramatically decrease costs.

When I evaluate companies that I'm asked to take over as CEO of, one of the counter-intuitive things I look for is a company that's really screwed up in a lot of obvious ways. Because, if the company has solid bones (like a good idea or customer base), once I fix the obviously wrong things, things will get better very quickly. That's low-hanging fruit and, by virtue of having the most expensive health care system in the world, we've got a *ton* of fruit to choose from.

Similar to the post-WWII virtuous cycle that helped created a golden age of American life, I'm optimistic that, by tackling our biggest issues, we can set off another golden age. As a series of fixes echo across our landscape, they will make sorting through them easier over time. Fixing the tax code using things like the VAT helps with our growing national debt, but also to "re-shore" jobs as it makes American manufacturing more competitive. This also helps increase healthcare coverage while decreasing costs, because a smartly designed program that gives universal basic coverage funded through the VAT, will drive down costs through payment reform and scale. Decreased healthcare costs will help defuse our long-term debt bomb in retiree-benefits, while the increased employment will create a larger pool to pay into the tax base.

Secure employment strengthens communities, which has positive effects on things like the drug epidemic. Like post-WWII prosperity, this positive flywheel means good begets good—as opposed to the negative spiral, where one negative leads to the other.

If you're deeply suspicious and negative on Trump, you can explain him that way, too. As the litany of issues piled up, they fed each other and spiraled, creating the perfect Petri dish for Trump to spring forward as an ideal (and credible) candidate for president.

Many smug Democrats look down on Trump and his supporters as being ignorant and uneducated to have fallen under his spell. Many smug Republicans see Trump as a fraud, impure on the three fundamental strains in the party: religious, libertarian, or neoconservative. His supporters sense this smugness and Trump has taken advantage of it to power his rise. As we so smugly ignored this witches' brew of issues that have vexed more than a hundred million Americans, Trump shoved it squarely back into view. We should thank him for that. We can get to work and fire him or hire him, but it's up to us to fix these totally solvable issues—or to shut up and stop complaining about President Trump.

The title of this book, *Decoding The Donald*, was largely figurative and tongue in cheek. I can't *truly* explain someone as colorful and unpredictable as Trump—I can only theorize. My subhead on the other hand ... *Trump's Apprenticeship in Politics* actually has a dual meaning that I *did* mean literally.

First, I do see this 2016 campaign as Trump's apprenticeship in politics, as he's now a contestant on a giant Reality TV show. Unlike my time on his show where he played judge, now there are millions of *You're Hired's* he needs to hear. His persona and experience have put him in the lead. Will that continue? I'm not sure, but, like millions of others, I can't look away.

The subhead also refers to *all* of this as a mirror. By holding a mirror to Trump's candidacy and understanding the context under which it exists and thrives, I hope watching *Trump's Apprenticeship in Politics* might be *our* wakeup call. I wonder if our collective reaction will be like that of an addict who goes to rehab because, when we look in the mirror, we're shocked into action by what we *finally* see staring back. I think of the saying "Sometimes you have to hit bottom," as I watch and wonder.

ACKNOWLEDGEMENTS

My mother. Just above her forehead, there's an indentation and a bump. When I was an infant, my parents were in a car accident. As my mom protected me in her arms, her head slammed against the dashboard. I note this because it exemplifies her lifelong selflessness. All my positive traits can be traced back to her.

Less sappy and more specific to this book, thanks also go to Jason Duff, Ittai Barzilay, Shekhar Kharnik, Jordan Pine, Nathan Dintenfass, Kristi Klemm, Kacie Kocher, Raman Seghal, Grace Kneapler, Tracy Michele, Rick Haelig, Sahil Lavingia, Howard Morgan, Dana Calvey, David Shaeffer, and Evan Solomon for reading early versions of this text and providing me with helpful feedback.

Many thanks also go to the fantastic Tiffany Wong for her terrific design skills on the cover and inside sketches. Thanks to Tom Pine for his careful copy editing on tight deadline.

All typos, errors, and omissions are strictly my own.

ABOUT THE AUTHOR

Donald Trump fired Surya back in 2006. Shortly after his misadventures on *The Apprentice*, Surya left his job as a brand manager at Procter & Gamble to work at some pre-IPO tech startups like LinkedIn and Groupon. In between, he ran for Congress in Southern Ohio. Despite a 4:1 funding disadvantage, he won his primary before losing in the general election. As the only major federal candidate in the 2010 cycle to refuse all special-interest money, his campaign was featured in the documentary, *Pay 2 Play*. Until its 2015 acquisition, he was CEO of civic-tech startup, PublicStuff. He currently lives in the Lower East Side of Manhattan. His best friend is Mr. Met.

[1] https://www.stormfront.org/forum/t1113497/

[2] Trump denies it, but it's a helluva coincidence if he didn't mean to be cute with his "blood coming out of her wherever" remark.

[3] http://www.politico.com/magazine/story/2015/11/days-of-desperation-213329

[4] http://nymag.com/daily/intelligencer/2016/01/trump-debate-boycott-throws-fox-news-into-chaos.html

[5] http://www.rollingstone.com/politics/news/how-roger-ailes-built-the-fox-news-fear-factory-20110525?page=13

[6] http://politicalticker.blogs.cnn.com/2011/08/16/christine-odonnell-witch-ad-was-a-mistake/

[7] http://mediamatters.org/research/2011/04/27/report-fox-promotes-birther-myth-in-at-least-52/179060

[8] http://www.theatlantic.com/magazine/archive/2016/01/the-great-republican-revolt/419118/

[9] It's possible Trump meant "their" and not "they're." As in *they're not ending their best. Their rapists* and not *they're rapists.* I have no idea, either way: obvi, no bueno.

[10] The only realistic hope was for the Supreme Court to strike down Obamacare, so Republicans couldn't be blamed. Unfortunately for them, it was twice upheld.

[11] http://www.nationalreview.com/article/422085/can-reconciliation-repeal-obamacare

[12] https://www.washingtonpost.com/blogs/fact-checker/post/when-did-mcconnell-say-he-wanted-to-make-obama-a-one-term-president/2012/09/24/79fd5cd8-0696-11e2-afff-d6c7f20a83bf_blog.html

[13] http://www.huffingtonpost.com/2014/12/19/congress-least-productive_n_6354762.html

[14] http://money.cnn.com/2015/05/18/news/economy/china-us-debt/

[15] https://en.wikipedia.org/wiki/List_of_the_largest_trading_partners_of_the_United_States

[16] http://www.nytimes.com/2012/08/19/business/new-wave-of-adept-robots-is-changing-global-industry.html?_r=1&pagewanted=all

[17] Robert Reich, *Aftershock,* page 53

[18] http://en.wikipedia.org/wiki/Report_on_Manufactures

[19] Beth Macy's, *Factory Man;* Kindle loc: 3092

[20] Beth Macy's, *Factory Man;* Kindle loc: 4300

[21] Read Michael Lewis' *Big Short* for a great overview. Or watch the movie!

[22] http://www.cnbc.com/2015/09/09/credit-card-debt-is-on-the-rise-.html

[23] http://www.csmonitor.com/Business/new-economy/2012/0609/Credit-card-debt-is-down-but-don-t-cheer

[24] http://www.calculatedriskblog.com/2016/01/fed-q3-household-debt-service-ratio.html?utm_source=feedburner&utm_medium=twitter&utm_campaign=Feed%3A+CalculatedRisk+%28Calculated+Risk%29

[25] http://finance.yahoo.com/q/pr?s=FB+Profile

[26] Beth Macy's, *Factory Man;* Kindle loc: 4499

[27] http://www.businessinsider.com/what-wall-street-protesters-are-so-angry-about-2011-10?op=1

[28] Beth Macy's *Factory Man;* Kindle loc: 4772

[29] http://crooksandliars.com/2016/01/new-cruz-ad-features-bankers-crossing

[30] http://www.bloomberg.com/politics/articles/2015-12-23/china-remains-vexing-campaign-test-for-presidential-candidates

[31] http://money.cnn.com/2015/05/26/news/economy/china-yuan-undervalued/

[32] January 2016

33

http://www.bis.doc.gov/defenseindustrialbaseprograms/osies/defmarketresearchrpts/techt
ransfer2prc.html
[34] http://online.wsj.com/article/SB10000872396390443295404577545440951791750.html
[35] https://en.wikipedia.org/wiki/SAIC-GM
[36] http://prestowitz.foreignpolicy.com/blog/12503?page=6
[37] http://www.nytimes.com/2012/01/22/business/apple-america-and-a-squeezed-middle-
class.html?_r=2&hpw=&pagewanted=all
38

http://www.themanufacturinginstitute.org/~/media/827DBC76533942679A15EF7067A70
4CD.ashx
[39] http://www.theatlantic.com/magazine/archive/2007/07/china-makes-the-world-
takes/305987/
[40] http://www.roanoke.com/multimedia/pickingup/
[41] http://www.politifact.com/truth-o-meter/statements/2015/oct/05/viral-image/fact-
checking-comparison-gun-deaths-and-terrorism-/
[42] http://www.brookings.edu/blogs/fixgov/posts/2016/01/01-trump-taking-advantage-of-
anxiety-mcelvein
[43] http://www.cnn.com/2015/06/01/politics/tsa-failed-undercover-airport-screening-tests/
[44] http://www.theguardian.com/technology/2015/sep/23/us-government-hack-stole-
fingerprints
[45] http://articles.baltimoresun.com/2012-09-06/news/bs-ed-sequestration-cyber-war-
20120906_1_cyber-attacks-sophisticated-cyber-cyber-warfare
[46] http://www.bbc.com/news/business-26609548
[47] http://www.usnews.com/news/articles/2015/09/24/are-china-and-russia-trying-to-
undermine-the-us-dollar
[48] http://www.telegraph.co.uk/finance/2773265/Billionaire-who-broke-the-Bank-of-
England.html
[49] https://en.wikipedia.org/wiki/Dwight_D._Eisenhower
[50] https://en.wikipedia.org/wiki/Eisenhower%27s_farewell_address
[51] https://www.washingtonpost.com/investigations/trumps-bad-bet-how-too-much-debt-
drove-his-biggest-casino-aground/2016/01/18/f67cedc2-9ac8-11e5-8917-
653b65c809eb_story.html
[52] http://money.cnn.com/2015/08/31/news/companies/donald-trump-bankruptcy/
[53] http://www.politifact.com/truth-o-meter/statements/2015/sep/21/carly-
fiorina/trumps-four-bankruptcies/
[54] http://en.wikipedia.org/wiki/United_States_public_debt
[55] http://www.treasurydirect.gov/govt/reports/pd/histdebt/histdebt_histo5.htm
[56] http://en.wikipedia.org/wiki/Financial_position_of_the_United_States
[57] http://en.wikipedia.org/wiki/Financial_position_of_the_United_States
[58] Solvable for America, anyway. A country like Japan, with no real immigration to speak of,
has no method to correct demographic issues.
[59] http://www.ontheissues.org/2016/Donald_Trump_Tax_Reform.htm
[60] http://www2.ucsc.edu/whorulesamerica/power/wealth.html
[61] http://www.nytimes.com/2012/08/15/business/economy/slipping-behind-because-of-
an-aversion-to-taxes.html?_r=1
[62] http://taxfoundation.org:81/article/number-words-internal-revenue-code-and-federal-
tax-regulations-1955-2005
[63] http://www.freedomworks.org/scrapthecode/topten.php
[64] http://www.nytimes.com%2F2015%2F12%2F30%2Fbusiness%2Feconomy%2Ffor-the-
wealthiest-private-tax-system-saves-them-billions.html
[65] http://money.cnn.com/2013/07/01/news/economy/corporate-tax-rate/
66

http://www.nytimes.com/2011/03/25/business/economy/25tax.html?_r=1&pagewanted=all
[67] http://www.nytimes.com/2012/04/29/business/apples-tax-strategy-aims-at-low-tax-states-and-nations.html?pagewanted=all
[68] http://www.bloomberg.com/news/articles/2015-07-22/tim-cook-s-181-billion-headache-apple-s-cash-held-overseas
[69] http://www.newyorker.com/magazine/2016/01/11/why-firms-are-fleeing
[70] http://www.wsj.com/articles/horizon-pharma-at-the-nexus-of-taxes-and-deals-1436296946
[71] https://www.nationalpriorities.org/budget-basics/federal-budget-101/spending/
[72] http://www.pgpf.org/chart-archive/0053_defense-comparison
[73] https://en.wikipedia.org/wiki/Military_budget_of_the_United_States
[74] http://www.pgpf.org/chart-archive/0053_defense-comparison
[75] http://papers.ssrn.com/sol3/papers.cfm?abstract_id=1375082
[76] http://www.bloomberg.com/news/2012-09-13/u-s-small-business-owners-say-candidates-don-t-get-their-needs.html
[77] http://www.ontheissues.org/Archive/America_We_Deserve_Health_Care.htm
[78] http://www.chcf.org/publications/2015/11/health-care-costs-101
[79] http://en.wikipedia.org/wiki/File:International_Comparison_-_Healthcare_spending_as_%25_GDP.png
[80] http://www.politico.com/news/stories/0512/75851.html
[81] http://en.wikipedia.org/wiki/Health_care_in_the_United_States
[82] http://content.healthaffairs.org/content/early/2008/07/29/hlthaff.27.5.w349.full.pdf+html
[83] http://content.healthaffairs.org/content/early/2008/02/26/hlthaff.27.2.w145.full.pdf+html
[84] http://www.newsweek.com/martin-shkreli-daraprim-drug-prices-374922
[85] http://www.rxrights.org/overview#.UFNtG6SXQig
[86] http://www.theatlantic.com/health/archive/2012/09/how-the-us-health-care-system-wastes-750-billion-annually/262106/
[87] http://www.kaiseredu.org/issue-modules/us-health-care-costs/background-brief.aspx
[88] http://www.newyorker.com/reporting/2012/08/13/120813fa_fact_gawande
[89] http://www.newyorker.com/reporting/2012/09/24/120924fa_fact_lepore
[90] http://www.paleycenter.org/p-the-nixon-kennedy-debates-a-look-at-the-myth/
[91] http://money.cnn.com/2015/12/06/media/donald-trump-nightly-news-coverage/
[92] https://www.opensecrets.org/lobby/
[93] https://www.opensecrets.org/lobby/top.php?indexType=c&showYear=2015
[94] http://graphics.wsj.com/elections/2016/how-trump-happened/
[95] https://www.washingtonpost.com/news/wonk/wp/2016/01/27/what-really-separates-trump-supporters-from-other-republicans/
[96] http://www.cnn.com/2015/12/22/politics/new-hampshire-2016-addiction/
[97] https://www.youtube.com/watch?v=StTqXEQ2l-Y
[98] Found again via Macy's Factory Man; Paper: http://economics.mit.edu/files/6341
[99] http://www.amazon.com/gp/product/B001ANYDJ0/
[100] http://www.salon.com/2012/09/26/robots_are_coming_for_your_job/
[101] http://www.gereports.com/post/115317859023/a-shortage-of-skilled-workers-threatens-manufacturings-r/

www.ingramcontent.com/pod-product-compliance
Lightning Source LLC
Chambersburg PA
CBHW032117280326
41933CB00009B/872